MICROCOMPUTERS

and the

3 R's

A Guide for Teachers

The Hayden Microcomputer Series

CONSUMER'S GUIDE TO PERSONAL COMPUTING AND MICROCOMPUTERS*
Stephen J. Freiberger and Paul Chew, Jr.

THE FIRST BOOK OF KIM†
Jim Butterfield, Stan Ockers, and Eric Rehnke

GAME PLAYING WITH BASIC
Donald D. Spencer

SMALL COMPUTER SYSTEMS HANDBOOK†
Sol Libes

HOW TO BUILD A COMPUTER-CONTROLLED ROBOT†
Tod Loofbourrow

HOW TO PROFIT FROM YOUR PERSONAL COMPUTER*
Ted Lewis

THE MIND APPLIANCE: HOME COMPUTER APPLICATIONS*
Ted Lewis

THE 6800 MICROPROCESSOR: A SELF-STUDY COURSE WITH APPLICATIONS*
Lance A. Leventhal

THE FIRST BOOK OF MICROCOMPUTERS
Robert Moody

MICROCOMPUTERS AND THE 3 R's: A Guide for Teachers*
Christine Doerr

DESIGNING MICROCOMPUTER SYSTEMS*
Udo W. Pooch and Rahul Chattergy

Consulting Editor: Ted Lewis, Oregon State University

†*Consulting Editor: Sol Libes, Amateur Computer Group of New Jersey and Union Technical Institute*

MICROCOMPUTERS

and the

3 R's*

A Guide for Teachers

*(Not to mention History, Social Studies, Biology, Foreign Languages, Political Science, Chemistry, . . .)

Christine Doerr

HAYDEN BOOK COMPANY, INC.
Rochelle Park, New Jersey

16284

To my parents, who taught me to strive
To my husband, who inspires me to achieve
To my children, who remind me that
the world is a beautiful place

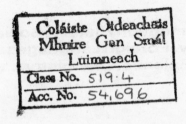
ISBN   0-8104-5113-1
Library of Congress Catalog Card Number   79-2443

        1   2   3   4   5   6   7   8   9   PRINTING

    79 80 81 82 83 84 85 86 87   YEAR

PREFACE

With the advent of the low-cost microcomputer, a new era has begun for teachers interested in using computers in their classrooms. No longer is instructional computing confined to schools with access to special-purpose federal funds. No longer will the purchase of a computer for general instructional purposes involve hundreds of thousands of dollars and require many years of planning by a variety of people. And no longer will the yearnings of individual teachers be overshadowed by the high cost and general complexity of computer systems. At last, average teachers with average students have the opportunity to augment their teaching effectiveness with this tool of technology.

This book was developed to acquaint the teacher who is a near novice (with regard to computers) with the wide range of computer and microcomputer applications that can be implemented at the secondary level. Such a teacher might have had a beginning programming class in college, but typically is not a very proficient programmer and is not knowledgeable about the uses of computers in education. The book is suitable as an individual reference or as the text of an introductory course for teachers and prospective teachers. As the teacher proceeds through the book, he or she will gain an understanding of the potential for computer usage in education while adding to his or her programming proficiency in the language called BASIC.

The book consists of three main sections. *Section I* contains a nontechnical discussion on microcomputers, their history, and capabilities; a summary and discussion of the benefits of using computers in the classroom; and practical and detailed hints on such preliminaries as configurations, location and setup, security, student and teacher reaction, and teacher training.

Section II provides an overview of the spectrum of educational computer use, with a chapter on each of the major types of instructional applications: computer science (Chapter 4), problem-solving (Chapter 5), simulations (Chapter 6), games (Chapter 7), and computer-assisted instruction (Chapter 8). Chapter 9 touches on simple administrative applications that might be of interest to a teacher or that could be used either in a very small school or for a single grade in a small- to medium-sized school. Chapter 4, on computer science, presents a syllabus for a course on "Computers and BASIC," as well as extensive Teacher's Notes that can serve as a self-instructional manual for the teacher who wants to learn BASIC.

Section III offers help and encouragement on two important fronts: One chapter lists instructional computing resources (organizations and publications), and the other provides first-level information on computer products available today, along with a discussion of the advantages of certain of their features.

Many high school teachers, if they consider the possibility of instructional computing, believe its benefits are restricted to the mathematics classroom. Not so. For each application type in Chapters 4–8, we include sample programs for other subjects: the hard sciences, life sciences, English, foreign language, history, or government.

Another common reaction of teachers is to be overwhelmed by all the possibilities of computer use and to be reluctant to get started because they believe they must immediately develop their own programs. Again, not so. A microcomputer can be used effectively in the classroom for many years without *any original program development ever being done by the teacher*. An incredible wealth of applications programmed in BASIC is already in the public domain. A great many of them run with little or no modification on any microcomputer supporting a reasonable level of BASIC (see Chapter 11 for a more detailed discussion).

Some highly respected people in the field believe that an individual teacher should not be encouraged or even allowed to experiment on his or her own with computers because the efforts might be inefficient, ineffective, or misdirected. Their argument is that if a school cannot afford to plan and implement an integrated program complete with a specially qualified staff, custom-tailored or developed programs, and adequate equipment, it shouldn't participate in a computer-aided program at all. We agree that a school-wide or district-wide program, with adequate resources, is an especially viable approach, mainly because experienced personnel can be hired and because more sophisticated equipment and software can be acquired. But we have seen too many successes result from the efforts of a single dedicated teacher to discourage others who might be equally successful.

We have not discussed the use of microcomputers to enhance an existing minicomputer or mainframe system. This will certainly be a very attractive application. In this situation, a microcomputer is used either as an intelligent terminal on-line to a larger system or as a multiplexor extending the power of an existing time-sharing system. We feel that this kind of hardware enhancement is beyond the scope of this book.

Microcomputer use in education is in the infant stage: We are just beginning to apply this new technology to age-old subjects and traditions. We hope you will join us in effectively applying this technological advance toward a very worthy goal: better education for our children and a better tomorrow for us all.

Good luck!

CHRISTINE DOERR

ACKNOWLEDGMENTS

I wish to express my gratitude to the people who contributed to the development of this book. To Ted Lewis, who talked me into the idea in the first place. To my husband, Jerry, who wrote or modified most of the programs, who provided invaluable technical consultation and scrupulous editing, and who had to live with me during the months in progress. To Bob Albrecht and Rick Meyer, who assured me I was on the right track. To my friends at Hewlett-Packard, who provided seemingly limitless reference material. And to the many members of the Hewlett-Packard Educational Users Group who helped me learn what I know about educational computing. Finally, to Maribeth McKinney, a good friend who does great typing.

CONTENTS

CHAPTER ONE

THE MICROCOMPUTER: WHAT IT IS AND WHAT IT AIN'T

Over the last five years, two electronic devices have found their way into a majority of American homes: the handheld calculator and the video game that hooks up to the family's television set. Within the next five years, these will be joined or superseded by a more comprehensive device that is both educational and recreational—the home computer.

Calculators have not only become a standard fixture in most homes, they have invaded the domain of the teacher, particularly in mathematics and science. You have only to scan the programs of conferences sponsored by professional organizations, such as the National Council of Teachers of Mathematics or the National Science Teachers Association, to perceive the level of concern about the effective use of calculators in the classroom. Most members of these organizations agree that these devices can add to a student's understanding of the subject when they are used correctly.

The same can be said about computers, except that because of their astronomical cost they have not spread as quickly through the educational system; and for the same reason they have not been the object of a "grass roots" movement starting in the students' homes. Now this situation has changed, with the introduction of the low-cost, easy-to-use microcomputer.

We can only imagine the events of the next few years, as the microcomputer settles into the nation's homes and moves into its schools. As more and more students have access to computers at home, the schools cannot afford to ignore the opportunities offered by these devices. Furthermore, there are sound pedagogical reasons for adopting the computer in the schools; the educational value of the computer has been discovered gradually over more than a decade of experience with larger, higher-cost computer systems. The impact of the calculator will seem minute compared to that we will experience as computer use in schools becomes commonplace.

1

Computers and Microcomputers

Let's take a look at this machine that has so suddenly become available to ordinary people and ordinary schools. How does it differ from the computer of the 1960s, and how has such a price breakthrough been achieved?

The *first generation of computers* was built using the vacuum tube as the primary electronic component. These early computers occupied several rooms with elaborate wiring and rigid environmental control. Then when the transistor, the integrated circuit (IC), and the printed circuit board were developed, so that many components could be connected on one board, computers could be made considerably smaller than before. Thus the *minicomputer* was born. It differed in two ways from larger computers built during the same era with this new technology: It had a smaller word size (16 as compared to 32 bits), and it offered less memory and less on-line storage. In other words, minicomputers were much smaller than their predecessors, but only slightly less capable; and for many applications the additional power was simply not needed.

In 1975, the first *microcomputer* was produced, and today's version differs from its big brothers in much the same way: It usually has a smaller word size (8 bits), less memory in the standard system, and a reduced capability for side (or peripheral) equipment. Again, the point is that the microcomputers are much smaller but only slightly less capable than computers that are much more expensive (Fig. 1-1).

For our purposes, we will define a *microcomputer* as a general-purpose computer that is small, not very expensive, and easy to use. There

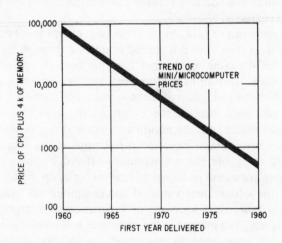

Fig. 1-1. Minicomputer/microcomputer price development.

are other, more technical, distinctions, but these three elements are crucial to the successful spread of computer applications in education. Just as the developments that enabled the birth of the minicomputer were also incorporated into larger machines of the time, within a few years most computers will be built around one or more microprocessors and could therefore technically be called microcomputers. However, we are addressing here a subset of microcomputers that is well suited to educational use.

Past Performance

In the past, computers have not entered the educational world at a very rapid pace. Certainly cost was a major factor: Besides the high purchase price of the computer itself, there was the cost of environmental support, such as air conditioning, and of structural changes in the computer room. But other factors contributed too: complex operating procedures, the lack of teacher training, no supporting curriculum, and the absence of significant research results.

Much to the credit of school personnel, impressive computer programs have been in existence in many of the country's metropolitan areas where there are enough students to support such an expensive endeavor or where there is federal support for special programs for underprivileged or underachieving students. Beyond these efforts, school districts in a number of areas have formed consortiums to share the costs of instructional computing. Administrative computing, mainly payroll and grade reporting, is nearly universal except in the very smallest and poorest districts. On the other hand, computer support for instruction or for the individual administrative needs of teachers has lagged far behind. Even where a program of instructional computing exists, the activities have been somewhat restricted by the still-too-high cost per student hour.

At last, computers are a possibility for all students in all schools. A computer system adequate for the computing needs of a typical class or small school can be bought for under $2,000, and this price is still decreasing. By 1980, we expect to see a computer priced well under $1,000 that will perform many educational tasks as well as computers selling in the mid-seventies could handle for a hundred times the cost.

The Breakthrough

The trend in electronic technology has been toward miniaturization. Technological advances leading up to the development of the microcomputer include the transistor, the printed circuit board, the integrated circuit, and finally the large-scale integration (LSI) chip. We won't describe these since they are incidental to our discussion.

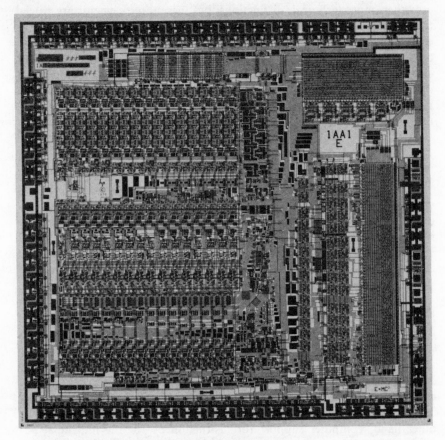

Fig. 1-2. Microprocessor chip. Actual size equals ⅜ inch. (*Courtesy* Hewlett Packard Journal)

The point is that the computer industry has been able to decrease progressively the size of the unit needed to accomplish a certain computational task. Today, the processor, which is the heart of any computer system, is smaller than a dime (Fig. 1-2). Decreased size alone has allowed decreased costs, but new materials and production techniques have been developed simultaneously that further lower the cost of building components. The result is that computers are smaller and cheaper now than anyone could have imagined thirty years ago.

Mix and Match—Parts of a Computer System

Regardless of size, every computer system has certain key parts:

1. *The Central Processing Unit (CPU).* This unit, the "brains" of the machine, controls the rest of the system components and performs the actual computations requested by the user's computer program.

2. *Memory* is used to store programs and data needed to carry out the user's instructions. Two terms you will hear describing memory are *core* and *semiconductor*. Most memories today are semiconductor; but since earlier memories were usually core, the words "core" and "memory" are often used interchangeably. Memory size is usually described in kilobytes (or thousand bytes, a byte being a small unit of memory). The unit kilobyte is often abbreviated "k"; thus, 4k of memory means 4 kilobytes or 4,000 bytes of memory. Later in the book we discuss the amount of memory needed for various activities. Two other terms relating to memory are important to you: ROM (read-only memory) and RAM (random-access memory).

a. ROM is a permanent unchangeable part of the system that contains programs supplied by the manufacturer to make it easier for you to use the computer. For instance, it takes care of all the set-up details that allow you to turn the computer on and immediately start programming. In some recent microcomputers, more and more ROM has been utilized, including putting the high-level language interpreter in ROM. Using ROM in this manner simplifies program start-up and leaves all your RAM available for program storage. Some companies also offer programmable ROMs (PROMs) and erasable PROMs (EPROMs) allowing you to store your own programs permanently.

b. RAM, on the other hand, is meant to be used to store the program you are currently working on or running, to store data needed during program execution, and to be "cleared" and reused whenever you wish.

3. *Mass Storage.* Usually only one program can reside in memory at one time. Thus, you need a way to store other programs and data files. For instance, if you have programmed ten games, the nine you are not currently using need to be stored. Without some means of storing them, each of them would have to be typed into the computer every time you wanted to run them. Two media are used for mass storage:

a. *Magnetic tape* (cassette size for microcomputers) is used with a specially adapted audio cassette player/recorder. The tape is read sequentially. For example, to find a program named HANG, the computer reads from the beginning of the tape, or wherever you arbitrarily start it, through all the programs until it finds HANG. This process can be time-consuming.

b. *Disk* storage (floppy disk for microcomputers) is faster than tape, since the disk can be accessed randomly. To find HANG stored on disk, the computer finds its disk location in a directory at a known place on the disk, then goes directly to that location. Also, disk storage is more dense than tape storage, so that data and programs can be stored in a smaller space. Unfortunately, disk is more expensive than tape, so that (even though the price is rapidly coming down) at this time it is hard to justify the added expense.

4. *Input/Output (I/O) Devices.* You also need some way to get programs into and out of the computer. A tape system or disk drive can be used for this purpose after programs have been written and stored; but you need a way to get new programs, new data, and program modifications into the computer. I/O for most computers is accomplished through some kind of terminal—teleprinter or CRT (video) terminal hooked up to the computer by cable or by telephone lines. The microcomputer relies almost exclusively on a simpler set-up—a keyboard and a video monitor.

Hard-copy printers are becoming available for microcomputer systems, although they are expensive and not needed for many school situations. Printers make economical sense only in cases of large program development (where a printed program listing is necessary to maintain the programmer's sanity), or where a good deal of record-keeping and written reports are necessary.

5. *Computer Programs.* All the equipment in the world won't yield any results without some way for you to tell the computer what to do—this is the function of the computer program. A *computer program* is a set of instructions that tell the computer what calculations to carry out and what to do with the results. These instructions are usually in a language "understood" by the computer—often a hard-to-decipher code. Increasingly, however, an English-like set of commands is "interpreted" by another program supplied by the manufacturer which is called, interestingly enough, an *interpreter*. The language most often found on microcomputers is BASIC (*B*eginner's *A*ll-purpose *S*ymbolic *I*nstruction *C*ode), although FORTRAN, APL, and some specialized educational languages are coming into use.

What Microcomputers Actually Look Like

Much like stereo sound systems, computers can be obtained either in a tidy, all-inclusive and fully portable package or in the more variable component form. Advantages are inherent in each approach.

The lowest-cost computers, in general, are self-contained. For example, the Commodore PET (the computer used to develop the programs for this book) looks like a TV screen with a keyboard joined to its front. Actually it includes a microprocessor CPU, 14k-bytes of ROM, 8k-bytes of RAM (a 4k version is also available), a cassette tape player/recorder, and the necessary interfaces to add other peripheral devices later, such as a

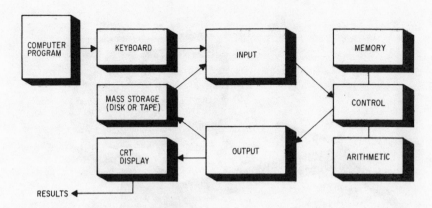

Fig. 1-3. Diagram of parts of a computer system.

printer or disk drive. The advantages to this system are its low cost, ease of use, and high reliability (Fig. 1-4).

Fig. 1-4. The Commodore PET 2001. (*Courtesy* Commodore Business Machines)

Fig. 1-5. The Sol-20 System. (*Courtesy* Processor Technology)

More comprehensive systems, appropriate for developing complex applications programs, are generally purchased in component form to allow the system to be "customized" for the application. For example a SOL-20 configuration might include a processor (one box), a video monitor (separate), a cassette player/recorder (specially adapted)or a disk drive, and a keyboard—all connected by cable and all manufactured by different companies. The advantages are that each component can be individually chosen by the user and that any selection of special-purpose devices (music or voice synthesizers, for instance) can be easily interfaced (connected) to the computer. In other words, using the analogy of the stereo system, the quality and flexibility of the component system can be "fine-tuned" to the needs of the user (Fig. 1-5).

Capabilities

With limitations, the microcomputer can do anything that any other computer can do; but, like other computers, it can do some things better than others. Its suitability for a particular application depends largely on its configuration. In the standard systems, microcomputers have less memory than minicomputers and large computers, but their memory can usually be expanded at relatively low cost. On the other hand, microcomputers are including more and more graphics capabilities, surpassing all but the most sophisticated of larger computers.

A microcomputer can play games with your students. It can supplement your math and science programs. It can add a new dimension to your language arts classes. As a teacher's helper, it can be a very patient tutor to students who need special help. It can also provide highly relevant vocational training. Administratively, it can compile athletic statistics, and it can keep class attendance and performance records. The limits to its contribution to your school lie in elements other than machine capability—that is, in teacher and administrative support, training, and curriculum development, to name a few.

Shortcomings

The primary difference in performance between microcomputers and larger systems is speed—both computer speed and peripheral speed. When microcomputers attempt a great deal of processing, their response time can be frustratingly slow. One cause of this lag is the smaller word size, which often necessitates more time to execute a given function. Another limitation of concern to educational users is the lack of time-sharing: A microcomputer system can support only a few users, and only a few relatively expensive microcomputer systems presently attempt time-sharing. Finally, a limited instruction set, in whatever language, is usually implemented on microcomputers. For instance, fairly powerful versions of BASIC are available, but they still usually omit some of the very useful features of Extended BASIC.

The Bottom Line

The microcomputer is well suited to the majority of all secondary level computing activities. It is at once an effective instructional aid, a supplementary record-keeping device, a valid object of instruction, and an exceptional means of presenting educational and recreational games. These capabilities, coupled with the low cost, will allow computers finally to be cost-effectively integrated into the curriculum of every school in the country.

References

PCC's Reference Book of Personal and Home Computing. Menlo Park, Cal.: People's Computer Company, 1977.

Cohen, Theodore J., "Microprocessors—A Primer," *Creative Computing* (September/October 1977).

Didday, Rich, *Home Computers: 2^{10} Questions and Answers* (Vol. 1: *Hardware*, Vol. 2: *Software*). Forest Grove, Oreg. 97116: dilithium Press, 1977.

Edwards, Judith L., ed., *Computers . . . A Beginning*. Corvallis, Oreg.: Continuing Education Publication, 1972.

Freiberger, Stephen and Paul Chew, *A Consumer's Guide to Personal Computing and Microcomputers*. Rochelle Park, N.J.: Hayden Book Co., Inc., 1978.

Libes, Sol, *Small Computer Systems Handbook*. Rochelle Park, N.J.: Hayden Book Co., Inc., 1978.

Miller, Merl and Charles Sippl, *Home Computers: A Beginner's Glossary and Guide*. Forest Grove, Oreg.: dilithium Press, 1978.

Moody, Robert, *The First Book of Microcomputers*. Rochelle Park, N.J.: Hayden Book Co., Inc., 1978.

Osborne, Adam, *An Introduction to Microprocessors* (Vol. 0: *For the Beginner*). P.O.Box 3026, Berkeley, Cal.: Osborne & Associates, 1977.

Waite, Mitchell and Michael Pardee, *Microcomputer Primer*. Indianapolis, Ind.: Howard W. Sams & Co., Inc., 1976.

White, James, *Your Home Computer*. Menlo Park, Cal.: Dymax, 1977.

CHAPTER TWO

WHAT THE MICROCOMPUTER OFFERS TO EDUCATION

Without doubt, the microcomputer is a milestone in computer technology—but what does it really have to do with secondary education?

Never before has computer access become so nearly a reality for so many schools. No longer will computer-aided learning be confined to large metropolitan school districts or to school systems with federal funds for special-purpose education. At last, the benefits of computer usage can be extended to smaller schools, ordinary student populations, and even the poorest districts.

In the first chapter, we very briefly described some of the activities that can be accomplished with a small computer, but we didn't make a clear case for adopting computer-assisted learning. In this chapter, we will discuss the benefits to be reaped from a computer-assisted learning program. Over the past ten years numerous studies have been carried out concerning the benefits of the various types of applications. We have synthesized their findings to give you this overview of the reasons for using computers in education.

Relevant Education

One of the battle cries in education in the last decade has been the need for "relevant" education. Students need to be prepared for their lives after graduation. They need instruction that will prepare them for what's ahead of them—higher education, a job, and everyday life, in whatever order—according to their personal choices.

Computer education can be the most relevant study in the high school curriculum. In the narrowest sense, students should learn about the capabilities of computers if only to understand the role of this marvelous machine in modern society and to protect themselves from possible computer abuse. If nothing else, the students of today should not feel helpless and conspired against when they receive inaccurate bills prepared by a computer. More generally, since the computer is becoming a tool in all phases of business, government, industry, and education, computer education is appropriate vocational training whether or not for a career in data processing. Being exposed to the construction and operation of a microcomputer, learning elementary high level language programming, and using this device to carry out classroom assignments is practical training for just about any future job. Finally, computers are being used in nearly every higher education discipline, and computer training at the secondary level provides a head start for effectively using computers in future study.

An Opportunity for Great Teaching

When teachers first consider a computer in their classroom, they are gripped by an all-too-common fear—the fear of being replaced by a machine. On the contrary, the computer *by itself* can never be as effective as a human teacher; an alliance of the two, however, creates a powerful teaching force. The computer, used creatively, has a multiplicative effect on the teacher's impact on his/her students. Far from threatening to replace *good* teaching, the computer offers a new arena with the opportunity for *great* teaching. To quote Thomas Dwyer, one of the veterans in educational computer usage:

> Put simply, I believe that computers in education are revolutionary because they make possible great teaching in a system dedicated to mass education. But they make this possible by supporting person-to-person educational influence, not by replacing it.*

Using the computer for instructional support—that is, as a tool for both teachers and students—frees them from the tedium of drill-and-practice work. Often, they become allies in the search for new facts and implications within their given subject. Teachers are freed from the negative roles as "judges," and they are free to expand their roles as mentors; yet at times the innovative student makes the breakthrough, providing the teacher with one of the great rewards in this profession.

Increased Student Motivation

Without exception, computers have been received enthusiastically by students of all interests and ability levels. In what is too often a boring environment, the computer is a novelty—yet this is one novelty that doesn't

*Thomas Dwyer, "Some Thoughts on Computers and Greatness in Teaching," *Topics in Instructional Computing*, Vol. 1, ACM Special Interest Group on Computer Uses in Education, 1975.

appear to wear off. When the computer is used as a problem-solving tool, students work harder than ever before to successfully program a solution. In computer-assisted instruction (CAI) situations, the nonthreatening and noncompetitive nature of the learning environment is a positive stimulus to the underachieving as well as to the average and above-average students. And when it comes to using simulations and games to reinforce the learning of key concepts and skills, students stop at nothing, even serious study, to "beat" the machine. Evidence of increased motivation is seen in attendance figures for students in classes where computers are used.*

Feedback

A critical factor in any learning situation, in school or not, is immediate feedback. Unfortunately, the average teacher cannot correct each paper within seconds of its completion. But the computer can and does. If the task is drill-and-practice on particular facts, the computer points out an error as soon as it is entered by the student, and presents another chance. Later, at the end of the lesson, the student is given a summary of his or her performance. When students are writing programs to solve a particular problem, natural consequences occur: The program won't work or the results of the program are unreasonable. In much the same way, when incorrect tactics are applied in simulations and games, a disastrous simulated outcome occurs or the student loses a scored event by an over-whelming margin. In all cases, this feedback is faster and more pertinent than that age-old standby, the red pencil.

Individualized Instruction

In individualized instruction lies one of the greatest promises of computer application to education—the chance to actually *increase* the rate of learning by allowing students to proceed at their own pace and by allowing teachers to make better use of their time.

For years, educators have dreamed of the day when instruction could be tailored to the needs of each and every student. At its best, individualized instruction allows each student to follow a course of study to the depth indicated by his or her interest and at the pace indicated by individual abilities, with easy access to one-to-one interaction with the teacher. But the teacher is often overwhelmed by the reality of the situation. Keeping track of thirty students at thirty different phases of the curriculum is in itself a full-time job; and pre- and post-testing chores to facilitate accurate diagnosis and prescription consume additional time. Add to that the challenge of preparing a wider range of materials than ever before, and

*"D.C. Secondary Schools Project for Computer-aided Education," *Hewlett-Packard Educational Users Group Newsletter* (May/June 1977).

you have a teacher in the midst of a nightmare rather than an enthusiastic tutor seeing a dream come true.

The computer can eliminate some elements of the nightmare by keeping records of student progress and by serving as a delivery vehicle for certain instructional activities.

The Case for Microcomputers

The microcomputer is about to make its mark on the educational world. A simple microcomputer system is well suited to meet the need for instructional computing in small schools or in particular areas of larger schools. Furthermore, the microcomputer can make a contribution, albeit a more limited one, in the area of administration. All the benefits of large-scale computers and time-sharing systems can be gained at least in part with a microcomputer, many without any sacrifice of scale. Within a very few years, in any case, distinctions between micro-, mini-, and conventional computers will be for the most part semantic. All computers will be built using microtechnology, and the size and configuration will be determined solely by the needs of the situation.

But at this time, the benefits of computer application to education can be attained at a significantly lower cost than any time in the past. Today, a complete microcomputer system can be bought for roughly the price of a 16-mm sound projector or a videotape unit, but it is more flexible than either of these instructional aids. At this writing, instructional computing can be delivered for roughly 18 cents per student hour; this figure is based on six hours of use per day through a 180-day school year for an estimated five-year useful life, and it includes repairs. This cost is about 20 percent of the most moderate estimates a year or two ago.

But cost alone doesn't make the microcomputer valuable in the average high school. Because these tiny computers can be located in the classroom, students can see their various parts, watch them work, and actually experiment with them. Accordingly, much of the mystique that now surrounds computers because of their size, expense, and delicacy will be dispelled.

A Change in Scope for Large Districts

Because of the microcomputer's attractive price/performance ratio, districts can afford to decentralize many of their computer services, while making more effective use of their larger system(s). A look at secondary level computer usage in 1975 revealed the following mix of instructional activities:*

*William J. Bukoski and Arthur L. Korotkin, "Computing Activities in Secondary Education," *Educational Technology* (January 1976).

Problem-solving	25%
Computer science	25%
Simulation and games	15%
CAI	13%
Guidance & counseling	15%
Other	7%
Total	100%

The same survey also shows that 62 percent of all instructional activities are programmed in BASIC, a language widely available on microcomputers. Here is the perfect arena for this little electronic wonder: By streaming off the problem-solving, much of the computer science, and a good portion of the simulation and gaming activities, the central computer is reserved for the instructional and administrative tasks that require powerful computation and extensive on-line storage (for instance, CAI, guidance, and student accounting). The student-controlled programming and simulation interaction is accomplished at an extremely low cost per student hour, with good response time sometimes not possible on the bigger machines simultaneously engaged in "number crunching" applications.

Even within a particular school, the cost of the microcomputer system makes it possible for an individual department to fund the purchase of a system for its exclusive use or even for use by a single classroom.

New Hope for Small Schools

Computer access has, for the most part, evaded the grasp of the small and typically rural school—for the simple reason that the initial cost was well beyond their already strained budget. The low-cost microcomputer opens the field to schools that are capable of only a small investment but that especially need the enrichment afforded by this unique tool. Often, school board approval is not needed for a medium-priced purchase; if it is, a strong case can be made for this capital investment. If worse comes to worst, an inexpensive computer could be financed by community fund-raising or by parental donations.

With Dreams Come Responsibilities

Widespread computer application to education has been a dream among a handful of people in education for many years. With the dawning of this dream comes the responsibility to maximize the well-known positive effects while minimizing the often feared problems that have been a concern since the beginning. These problems include dehumanization, invasion of student privacy, and the dangers of over-individualization. Like any tool, the computer can be abused, and the results can be disastrous. We believe, however, that these pitfalls can be adequately guarded against and that the benefits far outweigh the risks. The key lies in the quality of the people involved and the degree of commitment by both faculty and administration.

The computer can introduce a new dimension into high school education, one that is extraordinarily geared to the reality of students' future lives. As the information explosion continues, a shift must inevitably occur from the old style of education that stressed the acquisition of facts; what will be necessary in the world of tomorrow is increased skill in sorting and analyzing the vast quantities of available information. As the computer has been widely employed at this task in the realm of industry, so it can be liberating in education and in the student's personal life. The challenge for us is to expedite this liberation.

References

AEDS, *Layman's Guide to the Use of Computers*. Association for Educational Data Systems, 1201 16th Street, N.W., Washington, D.C. 20036.

Beck, C. H., "Growing Impact of Low-Cost Computers," *Intellect* (November 1976).

Bushnell, Donald D., *The Computer in American Education*. New York: John Wiley & Sons, Inc., 1967.

The following two documents can be ordered (75 cents each) from American Federation of Information Processing Societies, Inc., 210 Summit Ave., Montvale, N.J. 07645

Computer Education for Teachers in Secondary Schools: An Outline Guide (September 1971).

Computer Education for Teachers in Secondary Schools: Aims and Objectives (October 1973).

Computers in Education Resource Handbook. Eugene, Oreg.: University of Oregon, 1972.

Hicks, B. L. and S. Hunka, *The Teacher and the Computer*. Philadelphia, Pa.: W. B. Saunders Co., 1972.

Kibler, T. R. and P. B. Campbell, "Reading, Writing, and Computing: Skills of the Future," *Educational Technology* (September 1976).

Levien, Roger E., *et al.*, *The Emerging Technology: Instructional Uses of the Computer in Higher Education*. Hightstown, N.J.: McGraw-Hill, Inc., 1972.

Seidel, Robert J., *et al.*, *Learning Alternatives in the U.S.: Where Student and Computer Meet*. Englewood Cliffs, N.J.: Educational Technology Publications, 1975.

Tikhomirov, O. K., "Man and Computer: The Impact of Computer Technology on the Development of Psychological Processes," *National Social Studies Education Yearbook* (1974).

Zinn, Karl L., "An Evaluative Review of Uses of Computers in Instruction," *Project CLUE Final Report*, Office of Education, U.S. Department of HEW (December 1970).

CHAPTER THREE

HOW TO GET STARTED

We have answered certain fundamental questions about microcomputers and their use in the school. But a number of questions remain unanswered: What kind should you buy? Or should you build your own? Where should you put it? What will faculty reaction be? And what kind of training will teachers need in order to use it? In short, now that you know how useful a microcomputer can be in a school, how can you get started? This chapter deals with these practical concerns.

Build It or Buy It?

With all the publicity about the "home-brewed" computer system, the temptation is great for students and teachers jointly to build their own computer. We hope you can resist that temptation—except in isolated and carefully controlled situations. We recommend that you buy your microcomputer from a reliable and stable manufacturer. Also, when repairs are needed, take the computer to an authorized serviceperson. Our experience is that few teachers have the time or training needed to do an adequate job on these crucial tasks, and there is some danger in working with solid state components. Another argument for having repairs done professionally is that downtime can be highly detrimental to an instructional computing program: Students become frustrated and turned off by frequent system failures or shutdowns.

If one of the goals of the computing program is to teach students assembly skills and to give them practical operations experience, then we recommend that an additional microcomputer be bought in kit form to be put together, for instance, in either an electronics class or an elective computer science class. Complete stand-alone microcomputer kits are currently available for under $200; this price range allows students to have the unparalleled learning experience of actually building an electronic wizard, without delaying or jeopardizing the quality of the instructional computing program. In this type of program, maintenance and repair constitute just another challenge for students and teacher. Chapter 4 will give you some guidelines for carrying out the group assembly of the computer.

What Configuration Do You Need?

When deciding on the microcomputer to use in preparing this book, we looked for a number of features, first and foremost of which was a powerful version of the BASIC programming language. We needed character and string handling capabilities, SAVE and LOAD of named programs, built-in scientific functions, and multiple-dimensioned arrays. We also hoped it would have some graphic capabilities. In terms of hardware, we required a form of mass storage and the ability to add memory and peripherals, if needed at a later date. Equally important, we needed all these features at the lowest possible cost.

The choice was the Commodore PET, as shown in Figure 1-4. This computer system is completely enclosed in a sturdy, childproof case (a sturdiness we can personally attest to). The version of BASIC included in the ROM is adequate for our purposes, and the CRT screen editing procedures make it relatively painless to input programs. The large graphics character set was a bonus that we particularly appreciate for game-playing.

We reluctantly decided against a floppy disk system with an even more powerful BASIC (which was capable of formatted output and program overlay in addition to the other features), because speed wasn't particularly important and the dramatic price difference was. As the prices on disk drives continue to drop, they will become more and more attractive as the storage medium on most systems.

If you plan on running the BASIC application programs listed in this book, you need a configuration similar to our Commodore PET. If you plan to teach only assembler language or simplified BASIC programming, you can settle for a less comprehensive BASIC interpreter; settling for less, however, significantly reduces the overall usability of the machine.

Finally, if hard copy is needed for your specific application, you have the option either of adding a printer to your basic system or of buying a hard-copy terminal instead of the keyboard and low-cost TV monitor. Bear in mind that a good quality hard-copy device is an expensive acquisition, and sometimes it is so noisy that it can't co-exist in a classroom where students are listening or studying.

Where to Buy It

You really have only two choices for the source of your microcomputer: the manufacturer or a computer store. We don't have a decided preference for either.

If you are buying in quantity, either for a number of schools or for a widespread program in one school, you are better off buying directly from the manufacturer. For one thing, there is a quantity price break; for another, as a volume end-user you will have a certain amount of "pull" when it comes to warranty service (although the manufacturer will claim this is not true).

As a single computer user, you will probably do best to buy from a computer store if one is in your area. Unfortunately, these stores are still scarce outside of large metropolitan areas. If a store is close by, buying your computer there gives you a ready source of help with set-up and application problems. Even if you buy directly from the manufacturer, the computer store generally consults on programming problems or actually develops programs, if you are willing and able to pay for their services.

Once your computer is delivered, you should thoroughly check out all its capabilities. Read the documentation carefully, test the examples shown, and try other test cases that are a little different from the examples. We found several software "bugs" by trying to use certain features for cases more complicated than the simple examples in the documentation. It is important to discover any problems well within the warranty period for your system: Beyond that period, the manufacturer will probably not accept responsibility for "fixes," even when the problem arises from a design or implementation error.

Where to Put It

The computer can be physically integrated into an existing school in many ways. After all, our PET occupies only part of a card table, and its only physical support requirement is a 110-V grounded electrical outlet. For a school environment, however, there are some obvious logical restrictions on where you locate the computer.

Two elements are necessary for a successful instructional computing program: One is a conveniently located, highly reliable computer, and the other is a capable, enthusiastic teacher to direct the program. The computer should be kept in a place where the students for whom it is intended can easily access it for the planned program, and it should be available for their use before and after school. You have to provide the second element.

A Word about Security

Regardless of the setting, there is one potential problem with any microcomputer because of its size and portability: theft and, to a lesser degree, vandalism. The computer is extremely versatile within the school setting because it can be easily moved from place to place for use in various settings. But, unfortunately, it can also very easily be walked unobserved out of the school. Further, since the processor and all peripherals are either located adjacent to or encased with the keyboard or terminal, an act of vandalism can be catastrophic. Wherever the computer is in use, it should be under the continuous supervision of a faculty member or responsible student. At any other time, it should be under lock and key.

As important as the protection of the computer from student abuse is, the protection of the students from the high voltages of the box itself is even more important. If your hardware is not inside a protective case, you should install a plexiglass cover that allows students to observe the system components without their exposing themselves to any danger.

One Class—One Computer

In the ideal environment, each class participating in a computer-extended curriculum has its own computer. In many schools, each class picks up its own by accident, as a computing program gets started in one class and gradually spreads to other classes. A single system today is feasibly priced for use in one classroom and, with careful scheduling, can handle the computing needs of an entire class.

A mathematics or science class can keep a microcomputer busy continuously just for computational support; additional systems or slack time can be used for individual projects. Effective usage of the computer in the classroom is limited only by the knowledge and energy of the teacher: Teachers must be familiar with the equipment to begin with; they must quickly become intimate with it in order to stay ahead of the students. Above all, they must be totally convinced that it can, in fact, contribute to the quality of the student's learning experience.

The Portable Computer

Few environments are ideal, as we all know; and many schools will not experience the luxury of a computer in every classroom for some years. In these schools, a compromise can be reached by sharing the computer among several classrooms and several subjects during the school year. Many schools begin their programs this way and later add more computers as their budgets and expertise grow. In this type of program, the computer might start the year in the mathematics class, move to the history class after Christmas, and finish the year in the physics laboratory. The computing activities within each classroom can be assigned at the discretion of the teacher, or they can be part of a cooperative program carefully developed by one or more of the participating departments.

In a variation of this rotating program, the computer can rotate among several schools, as part of a district-wide program for selected students—gifted or handicapped, for example.

Directed Individual Activity

Rather than use the computer uniformly for all students in one classroom, some schools use it in an individualized study program. In such a case, it is used in vastly different ways for different groups of students from the same class or for individual students from a number of classes. For instance, it might be used for special projects by advanced or honors students, while also being used as a motivational tool by underachieving or indifferent students. When the computer is used for this kind of program, it should be located outside the classroom, either in a separate computer room (supervised by an aide or student helper) or in a room adjacent to the classroom of the teacher most familiar with the machine (a room accessed only through the classroom for security). Students can then use the computer during their free periods, with machine time scheduled in advance or simply used on a first-come-first-served basis. If someone is not always on hand to answer questions and help with problems (as in the adjacent room setup), regularly scheduled help sessions should be made available.

Free Access Computing

In the most innovative of schools, the computer can be a free access resource available to any student in the school for whatever activity he or she chooses. Accordingly, the computer would be located in a very public place—in an easily reached computer room off a main classroom, in a library, or in a resource center. As always, a knowledgeable person should be available at all times to answer questions about the machine and about BASIC programming, as well as to suggest the use of the school's library of "canned" programs stored on tape or disk.

When individual students take up computer time for directed activity, certain hours of the day (or before and after school) might be designated for free access computing. There is considerable merit in merely exposing a large number of students to the incredible world of computing, even if exclusively through the use of computer games. You will have to be careful to keep a fixated few "computer freaks" (student or faculty!) from monopolizing the computer during these free hours.

Student Computer Club

In some instances, the school microcomputer is bought and assembled by members of a computer club, usually to supplement other computing equipment already available. In such a case, the microcomputer can be located in the existing computer room or in the classroom of the club advisor. Before and after school use would most likely be restricted to club members, but the system can be available during the day for general school use.

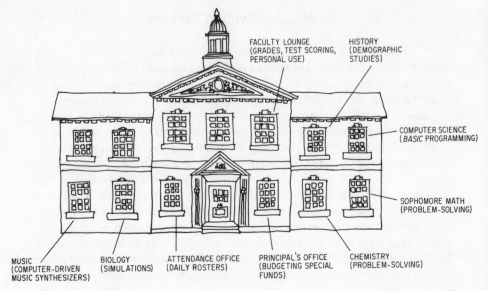

FACULTY LOUNGE
(GRADES, TEST SCORING,
PERSONAL USE)

HISTORY
(DEMOGRAPHIC
STUDIES)

COMPUTER SCIENCE
(*BASIC* PROGRAMMING)

SOPHOMORE MATH
(PROBLEM-SOLVING)

MUSIC
(COMPUTER-DRIVEN
MUSIC SYNTHESIZERS)

BIOLOGY
(SIMULATIONS)

ATTENDANCE OFFICE
(DAILY ROSTERS)

PRINCIPAL'S OFFICE
(BUDGETING SPECIAL
FUNDS)

CHEMISTRY
(PROBLEM-SOLVING)

Fig. 3-1. A projection of microcomputer distribution as it might appear in several years.

The Future

Figure 3–1 is a projection of microcomputer distribution as it might occur several years from now. All the applications shown are possible today, and they are discussed in detail in later chapters. However, at present, large-scale usage as depicted in the diagram is nonexistent because of budgetary constraints and a general skepticism about the value of computers in education. By the mid-1980s two phenomena will have occurred to minimize these restrictive factors: (1) more sophisticated and more capable equipment will be available at much lower costs, and (2) "computer awareness" will have spread throughout a larger portion of our society. Increasingly complex educational applications will be implemented on low-cost systems, and resistance among teachers, parents, and administrators to educational computing in general will be lessened.

Student Reaction—and How to Exploit It

Student reaction to computers in the school is almost universally positive. Even those who are initially threatened by the computer quickly become intrigued. One word of warning: the room in which the computer is located becomes the Mecca for computer enthusiasts among both student body and faculty. Almost before the computer is installed, a colony of "computer freaks" forms whose members invariably spend every spare minute in the computer room. If the teacher with custody of the machine properly nurtures and manages this devotion, these students can do a large portion of the school's program development.

How can the teacher bring about such a miracle? By encouraging the students' interest, by providing them with high-level design specifications, and by offering abundant help along the way, the instructor finds they are amazingly productive and ecstatic when given a "real" problem to solve. Besides being mutually satisfying to both parties, the experience is valuable vocational training for this group of talented students who might eventually pursue a career in computer science.

Teacher Reaction—and How to Overcome It

Every school has at least one teacher who is an enthusiastic advocate of computers. The first computer in the school usually winds up in this teacher's classroom or at least under his or her direction. Many of the other teachers feel threatened by this demon of technology that they neither understand nor want to understand. Even as the enthusiasm of the computer advocate spreads to teachers occupying the middle ground between these two positions, the hard-core resisters still require several levels of persuasion before they will even think of using a computer in their classes.

The five types of training experience that should be made available to all teachers according to their interests or needs are as follows:

1. Continuing Education. In a very broad sense, every secondary teacher needs to have some degree of computer literacy, whether or not the teacher is likely to actively use a computer in the classroom. Many colleges and universities now offer an undergraduate "Computers in Education" course, where teachers-to-be and returning teachers learn some of the ways computers are used in the educational process. They also often learn how to program in a high-level programming language such as BASIC. Such a class helps to relieve the anxiety of the teacher on the arrival of the computer.

2. Direct Contact with the "Spark Plug." The next level of teacher training occurs quite naturally from direct contact with the computer advocate. A few interested teachers seek the enthusiast out to find out what he or she is doing with the new arrival and to determine which activities might be applicable in their own classes. This contact might prompt them to request computer time for their classes, to ask that the computer be rotated to their classrooms for some period of time, or even to enroll in an upper division college course in computer programming or computer applications to learning.

3. In-Service Courses. The school or district should also make available in-service courses to help new computer users bridge the gap between literacy and implementation. Some possible courses are BASIC programming, machine language programming, and short courses on specific types of applications (problem-solving, simulation, games, and the like).

4. Operations Training. At the very least, any teacher who wants to begin using the computer in the classroom needs to learn how to run it. This can be accomplished by informal contact with the computer advocate or in a small structured class at a convenient time, such as after school.

5. Release Time. Once teachers are enthused about the computer's possibilities, they need time to develop or modify curriculum to fit their particular needs. Ideally, each should be given one or two periods per day of release time from teaching duties for one or more quarters. Not many schools, unfortunately, are able to be this generous; luckily, due to the dedication of many teachers involved in computing, the curriculum is developed anyway, at the expense of their evenings and weekends.

As microcomputer usage proliferates, a more enlightened attitude toward program development may evolve in the schools.

Plug It In and Go

This chapter has outlined various ways in which the microcomputer can be introduced into a school environment. It has listed several possible program organizations. And it has described a hierarchy of teacher training that prepares teachers to integrate the computer into their teaching. Even with this much planning, there comes a time when you have to plug in the machine and start using it. But how?

This book provides a collection of applications, already programmed in BASIC, that allow teachers in several different subjects to start using the computer without any preparation other than simple operations training. Many more applications are available in the listed references. These applications will not fit every situation, but they are a foundation on which to build a more comprehensive program, and they will keep the machine in use and students busy during the months it takes dedicated teachers to tailor other educational applications to their special needs and to the capabilities of their particular machines.

References

Bass, C. C., Dean Brown, and E. Nold, "Computers and Teacher Education," *Educational Technology* (September 1975).

Emmerick, Paul J., "Teachers, Student Teachers, and Computing," *The Journal* (December 1975).

Lunetta, Vincent N., "Computer in the Classroom: A Unit in Teacher Education," *Journal of Educational Technology Systems* (Spring 1975).

Milner, Stuart D., ed., *Topics in Instructional Computing, Vol 1: Teacher Education*, a special ACM SIGCUE publication (January 1975). Order from SIGCUE, Kiewit Computation Center, Dartmouth College, Hanover, N.H. 03755 ($4).

CHAPTER FOUR

COMPUTER SCIENCE

This chapter is divided into several parts: *First*, a course syllabus outlines a class in "Computers and BASIC Programming." *Second*, Teacher's Notes for the syllabus, including a brief description of the main statements and commands in BASIC, serve adequately as a first-level reference for teaching the course. (At the end of the chapter, we list more detailed references.) These Notes can also serve as a self-instructional introduction to BASIC for the teacher who does not know the language but who wants to learn how to program in it. *Third*, the enhancements available on the PET machine are described so that the programs in this book can be deciphered by people familiar with a different BASIC interpreter. *Fourth*, problems, for use with the syllabus or by themselves, are categorized according to the statements you need to know in order to program the solutions. *Fifth*, we include a few hints for teachers leading their students through building a computer from a kit. (If the computer does not support BASIC, another text or manual is necessary to learn to program in machine language.) *Finally*, a list of topics is given that might be offered in an advanced programming course for those students who wish to continue their computer science study.

A Note on Computer Literacy

In 1972, the Conference Board of the Mathematical Sciences recommended that a course in computer literacy be introduced at the junior high level for all students. We all hope the day will soon arrive that such a widespread availability is possible. However, right now your students probably have not had a class in which they learned a little about the capabilities of computers, how they are used in our society, what they cannot do, and so forth. If so, we suggest that you precede the "Computers and BASIC" course with a short literacy course. There are two excellent books on computer literacy:

Ball, Marion, *What Is a Computer?* New York: Houghton-Mifflin Co., 1972.

Rice, Jean, *My Friend the Computer*. Minneapolis, Minn.: T.S. Dennison Co., 1976.

Or, if you wish to combine a literacy course with a very general and easy-going introduction to BASIC, the following three books are recommended:

Albrecht, Bob, *My Computer Likes Me When I Speak BASIC*. Dymax, 1972.

Dwyer, Tom, *A Guided Tour of Computer Programming in BASIC*. Houghton-Mifflin Co., 1973.

Simon, David E., *BASIC from the Ground Up*. Hayden Book Co., Inc., 1978.

If you use any one of these books for a preliminary course, you will need to modify the course syllabus to eliminate overlap.

A Course in Computers and BASIC

The following course syllabus is designed for seven weeks of instruction, with three one-hour sessions per week. We suggest a maximum ratio of four students working at each computer/terminal at a time; group usage often works out quite well, with the four students learning from each other. If your situation does not permit this ratio, then laboratory time has to be carefully scheduled to give everyone a chance to do assignments. For example, if you have twenty students and only one computer, you need to schedule five lab sessions for each one suggested in this section.

If your computer system interfaces with a closed circuit TV monitor, so that you can demonstrate features of BASIC to the class as a whole, by all means use this capability. It makes teaching easier, and the students find it easier to understand. Otherwise, make liberal use of the blackboard.

You will notice that the course includes some elements of computer literacy instruction. We think a successful introduction to computers must present some general concepts and assertions about computers and their uses. If for some reason this aspect of the course is inappropriate in your situation, week six can be deleted.

Week One: Getting Acquainted with the Computer

Session 1: Lab. Give instructions on how to LOAD and RUN programs, then let the students randomly access the collection of games you have for your computer.

Session 2: Lecture. Discuss the similarities and differences of calculators and computers, describe the parts of a computer and their functions, and introduce the concept of programming and languages (machine-level as compared to high-level). Play "computer," with students carrying out the functions of the various components.

Session 3: Class Discussion. Discuss some of the uses of computers in our society.

Week Two: Getting Ready to Write Programs

Session 1: Lecture. Describe computer programs and their purpose, define algorithms, and introduce flowcharting as a method of representing algorithms. Assign several flowcharting exercises as homework.

Session 2: Lecture/Lab. Describe data types, variables, and the PRINT, LET, INPUT, and END statements. Have the students try these out at the computer.

Session 3: Lecture/Lab. Describe the use of statement numbers and explain the commands NEW, LIST, and RUN. Assign several simple programming problems to be done in class.

Week Three: Writing Programs

Session 1: Discussion/Lab. Assign more programming problems to be worked on in class. Discuss any trouble students might have had with the first set and review the statements as necessary.

Session 2: Lecture/Lab. Discuss the concepts of conditional operations and looping. Describe IF...THEN and GOTO statements. Assign several simple programs demonstrating these statements.

Session 3: Lecture/Lab. Briefly review the topics of the previous session, especially the IF...THEN and GOTO statements. Then describe the FOR...NEXT statement. Assign more programs that use these statements.

Week Four: More Programs

Session 1: Lecture/Lab. Describe READ, DATA, and the functions SQR, ABS, SGN, INT, and RND. Assign exercises that demonstrate the use of these statements and functions.

Session 2: Lecture/Lab. First describe the DIM and MAT instructions that are available with your version of BASIC. Then discuss debugging procedures and standards for program documentation. Assign a program to be written using the statements, and require that it be debugged and properly documented.

Session 3: Lecture/Lab. Discuss the use of subroutines. Then assign a program that incorporates this week's statements with those already learned.

Week Five: Lab Wrap-up

Session 1: Lecture. Introduce more advanced computer concepts—number representation (binary, octal, hexadecimal), ASCII and EBCDIC codes, time-sharing, and peripherals. If you are unfamiliar with these concepts, you can either delete this session or bone up from a computer science text such as *Minicomputers: Structure and Programming* by T. G. Lewis and J. W. Doerr (Hayden Book Company, Inc., 1976.)

Session 2: Lecture/Lab. Discuss the capabilities of formatted output if available with your BASIC. Assign simple exercises that demonstrate this capability. Assign a final project to be completed by the end of the course.

Session 3: Lecture/Lab. Discuss the enhancements and limitations that are unique to your machine. Let the students experiment with these enhancements. Any remaining time should be spent working on the final projects and answering any questions.

Week Six: Expanding Student Literacy

Session 1: Lecture/Lab. Discuss in detail the contributions of computers to society in government, in business and industry, and in education. Lab time should be spent working on the final projects.

Session 2: Lecture/Lab. Discuss the potential hazards of massive computer dependence in our society. Lab time should, again, be spent working on the final projects.

Session 3: Lecture/Lab. Discuss the vocational implications of computers. Lab time as before.

Week Seven: Computers, the Present and the Future

Session 1: Lecture/Lab. Discuss computers and the future. Lab time is to be spent finishing up the final projects.

Session 2: Field Trip. Arrange to visit a local computer store, have the owner or manager present a talk on available products, and let the students try out the different systems. Have the students turn in their final projects when you return to school.

Session 3: Class Discussion. Discuss the work done on the final projects and answer any questions that come up. For interested students, discuss any follow-up courses that are available either in the school or elsewhere (perhaps adult education), books and periodicals that might be helpful in nourishing their interest, and so forth. If time permits, demonstrate some of the more interesting programs written as projects.

Teacher's Notes on Computers and BASIC

This section contains suggestions for how to handle some of the lectures and discussions outlined in the course syllabus, and it also provides a brief description of the statements referenced there. Reading this section should be adequate (though perhaps rigorous) preparation for the novice to begin programming in BASIC; and it serves as a concise review for those already conversant in the language.

Week One

Session 1. Write the LOAD and RUN instruction formats on the blackboard for student reference. List a directory of games available on your machine. Explain how to stop an executing program (generally by pushing the Break or Stop key, or in some cases a control C); also pre-explain messages the students might receive from the computer if they mistype an instruction (SYNTAX ERROR) or if they enter an unintelligible response (REDO FROM START on our PET).

A games session like this is quite valuable for several reasons: It familiarizes students with the computer and the most elementary method of using it; it dispels any fears they might be harboring about the machine; and it makes them interested in the course content.

Session 2. Start this session by defining a computer and generalizing its capabilities; for example, you can compare it to a fifth-grade arithmetic genius who is incapable of learning inductive reasoning.

Then try to define a boundary between calculators and computers, as hazy as the distinction often is. Nonprogrammable calculators are easily differentiated from computers by the obvious fact that they are not programmable. However, many simple problems don't require a computer, and in fact they should be done on a calculator rather than on the unnecessary and complicated computer. For instance, to calculate the price of a quarter-pound of tomatoes if 2 pounds cost $1.39, use a calculator. But to calculate the cost of a quarter-pound of each of 1,000 items, including an 8 percent discount and a 6½ percent sales tax rate, the use of a computer or programmable calculator would be advisable.

We arbitrarily set three differences between calculators and computers that are currently applicable (though there are bound to be exceptions!):

1. *Memory Size and Expandability.* A calculator typically has several hundred memory locations, whereas a computer has several thousand. In addition, computer memory is usually expandable; in other words, if, say, 8,000 locations can be bought initially, more locations can be added later—up to 32,000, 64,000, or even more

on some machines. Programmable calculator memory is typically not expandable.

2. *Speed*. As a rough example, most calculators take roughly a second to calculate the SIN function, whereas a computer completes that function usually ten times that fast.

3. *Use of Peripherals*. Some programmable calculators are now available with small tape printing devices, but computers can use larger printers, CRTs, mass storage devices (disks, tapes, and the like), and other special-purpose peripherals.

Introduce the concept of *programming* in a "machine language." In general, *machine language* is very detailed and takes a lot of statements to accomplish a small task. Many people prefer to program in what is called a *high-level language* (like BASIC)—usually an English-like set of statements and commands, each of which accomplishes a task that would take several machine statements. Different high-level languages are used in different environments: COBOL for business programming, FORTRAN for scientific programming, and BASIC for general purpose and educational applications.

Assign students to play the parts of a computer, and have them solve simple problems by going through the steps that a computer has to perform:

> Human gives problem to Input
> Input sends to Memory
> Human gives RUN to Input
> Input gives RUN to Control
> Control fetches problem from Memory
> Control sends problem to Arithmetic
> Arithmetic computes and sends answer to Control
> Control gives answer to Output
> Output tells Human the answer

Session 3. Lead a class discussion of some of the uses of computers in our society. Solicit as many applications from students as they can think of: airline reservations, checking account records, check verification machines in supermarkets, product labeling in retail stores, invoicing by major department stores, "personalized" letters from charitable organizations, and so on. Discuss some of the computations that computers can make and that students are familiar with—computing pi, solving equations, printing report cards, and tabulating election results, for example. Emphasize that the computer is a tool of man, merely a slave to the people who program it: it doesn't think. Explore the recreational possibilities vis-à-vis the games played in Session 1.

Week Two

Session 1. Describe a computer program and emphasize the fact that the computer does *exactly* what it is told, never more or less. It doesn't "know what you mean" as a teacher might if a student used 3.13 as the value of pi instead of 3.14.

Define an *algorithm* as a sequence of steps that if given proper input, arrives at the solution to a problem. Lead from there into flowcharting as a method of representing an algorithm. Use "standard" flowcharting symbols, as shown in Fig. 4–1. As a class activity, flowchart together several commonplace activities such as driving to the store, getting ready for school, and similar activities. Then flowchart a few simple mathematical or scientific problems. The example in Fig. 4–1 would be a good start. Then try $Y = 119 - 33/5 + \sqrt{8}$; $Y = X^2 + 3X + 5$ for $X = 25$. Then discuss the value of flowcharting as an aid in designing programs. In other words, an algorithm is developed to solve a problem, and a flowchart is designed to represent the algorithm. The flowchart is then converted to a program.

Assign a moderately difficult topic from your subject matter to be flowcharted for the next class.

Session 2. Describe the two data types:

1. *Numeric values* are those with which most students are familiar, such as 3, .001, −757.41, and the like. BASIC usually allows a type of scientific notation such as 3.897 E2 which means 3.897×10^2, or 389.7.

2. *String values* are collections of characters, sometimes delineated by quotes, such as "ABCDE," "MY NAME IS," "AB...+...WOW." Your BASIC may or may not permit inclusion of a quote symbol itself as part of a string. Also note that a string may be defined as having no characters, and it is therefore represented as input by two quotes together: " "

Describe variables:

1. *Numeric variable* names are one or more characters, the first of which must be a letter and the rest of which must be letters or numeric digits. However, most BASICs use only the first two characters to determine the uniqueness of a variable. In the examples A, A1, A2, VC, HIGH, LOW, PRIME, XA1, XA2, note that XA1 and XA2 are indistinguishable to BASIC.

2. *String variable* names follow the same rules as numeric variable names, except that a $ must be added at the end of the name. In the examples A$, NAME$, CITY$, GAME$, GANG$, note that GAME$ and GANG$ are indistinguishable.

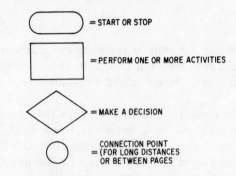

AN EXAMPLE:
TO REPETITIVELY DETERMINE AND PRINT WHICH OF TWO NUMBERS (X AND Y)
IS CLOSEST IN VALUE TO A THIRD NUMBER (A), AND TO STOP IF A = O, THE
SYMBOLS WOULD BE USED THUS:

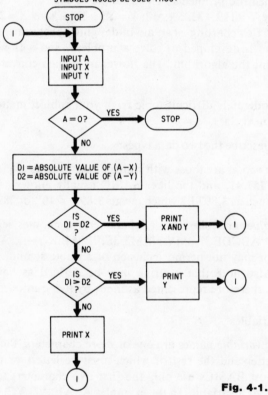

Fig. 4-1.

Describe numeric operators and the precedence of operators:

　　1. *Numeric operators* are + (addition), − (subtraction), *
(multiplication), / (division), ↑ (exponentiation).

　　2. The *precedence of operators* is as in algebra: first is ↑; second are
* and / in the order they are encountered; and last are + and − in the order

they are encountered. Precedence can be overridden by the use of parentheses. For example:

$$2 + 3 * 4 \text{ is } 14$$
$$(2 + 3) * 4 \text{ is } 20$$
$$2 \uparrow 3 - 4/5 \text{ is } 7.2$$
$$2 \uparrow (3 - 4)/5 \text{ is } .1$$

Describe the use of the statements PRINT, LET, INPUT, and END. (Note that you signal BASIC that you have completed the entry of each statement by pushing a Carriage Return key or its equivalent on your system.)

1. A *PRINT statement* consists of the word PRINT followed by the list of items (any mix of numeric or string values) to be printed. In general, PRINT P_1, P_2, ... P_n causes the n listed strings, numbers, or expressions to be printed on the printer or CRT. If $n = 0$ (that is, if nothing follows the word PRINT), a blank line is printed. Assuming $X = 5$, examples are:

Statement	Resulting printout
PRINT 5.2	5.2
PRINT "HELLO"	HELLO
PRINT	
PRINT 3*2↑(3 + 1)	48
PRINT "3*2↑(3 + 1)"	3*2↑(3 + 1)
PRINT "VALUE IS", 3.2	VALUE IS 3.2
PRINT X, "TIMES 3 IS", X*3	5 TIMES 3 IS 15

If you try these on your computer, you'll probably find there are some predefined "tab" settings that determine where each P_i is printed. Your BASIC may allow you to replace the commas with semicolons between the P_is to override the tabs and cause the P_is to be printed closer together; check the effect on numbers and strings on your computer. Whereas each PRINT normally starts printing on a new line, placing a semicolon after P_n suppresses the advancement to a new line, with the result that a subsequent PRINT starts on the same line as the one on which the last PRINT stopped.

2. *LET* is used to assign values to variables. For example:

LET X = 33
LET Z = 3↑(X/5) + 14
LET Y$ = "COMPUTER"

On most microcomputers, you don't even have to include the word LET—the statement X = 33 is interpreted as LET X = 33.

3. *INPUT* is used to elicit and accept input from the person sitting at the keyboard. It can thus be used to first print a request for data and then accept the answer. Examples:

INPUT X	The computer prints a ? and waits for a numeric value to be input.
INPUT X$	The computer prints a ? and waits for a string to be input.
INPUT "WHAT IS THE VALUE OF X"; X	The computer prints WHAT IS THE VALUE OF X? and waits for a number to be input.
INPUT "WHAT IS YOUR NAME"; X$	The computer prints WHAT IS YOUR NAME? and waits for a string to be entered.

4. The *END statement* should be the last statement in a program; on the PET and many others, its use is not mandatory.

Session 3. Describe statement numbers, the commands NEW, LIST, and RUN, and error messages.

As you may have noted earlier with the PRINT statement, typing a statement without a preceding statement number causes the statement to be executed immediately. If preceded by a statement number, the statement is stored in memory for later execution. Statement numbers can be 1 through 9999 or more, depending on your BASIC. Since a program consists of a set of numbered statements that are executed sequentially, it is usually numbered by tens so that a forgotten statement can be entered later without renumbering all subsequent statements. Entering a statement number with no statement causes the deletion of any previously entered statement with that number.

1. Before entering a new program, type NEW followed by a Carriage Return. This procedure deletes all previously entered statements from memory.

2. At any time, the program can be listed by typing LIST followed by a Carriage Return. Most BASICs allow some method to list only part of the program.

3. The command RUN is used to start executing the program currently in memory, in order by statement number. Running only a specified part of a program is possible, as long as that part is complete in itself.

RUN	The program in memory is executed starting at the lowest numbered statement.
RUN 99	The program is executed starting at statement 99.

4. Error messages are printed out by BASIC when something "illegal" is done. For instance, you may already have seen something like "SYNTAX ERROR" if you typed PRNT instead of PRINT. A list and corresponding explanations should be given for the error messages on your computer.

Assign several simple programming problems to be done in class. A list is provided in the next section of this chapter.

Week Three

Session 1. Review the statements already discussed, and answer questions that might have come up. Write the programs for some of the assigned problems on the blackboard and explain each step.

Session 2. Conditional operations and looping represent the real power of computers, and they are concepts often difficult for students to grasp. Reexamine the flowcharts generated earlier in the class, emphasizing the decision points. If no loops were used, introduce some now. Try this problem as an example: Find the sum of all integers between 1 and 1,000. (The flowchart for this problem is in Fig. 4–2.)

Discuss the five parts of a generalized loop:

1. initialization of the loop variable,
2. processing within the loop,
3. adjustment of the loop variable,
4. testing of the loop variable, and
5 branching (that is, changing the natural flow direction) to the top of the loop depending on the loop variable.

Point out each of the five parts in Fig. 4–2. Note that not all loops have parts 1 and 3, as in, for instance, a program that loops until a particular input is encountered. See Fig. 4–1 for an example of this.

Now introduce the GOTO and IF...THEN statements.

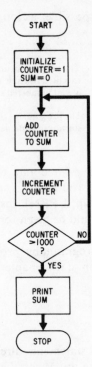

Fig. 4-2.

1. *GOTO* is simply a statement that changes the normal flow of the program. The form is GOTO followed by a statement number, which can be greater than, smaller than, or even the same as the statement number of the GOTO itself. Example:

GOTO 150
The computer immediately
moves to statement number 150
and continues from there.

Unfortunately, a variable for the statement number (as in GOTO N) is usually not allowed.

2. *IF...THEN* allows for a test and then an action only if the test is true. If the test is not true, the computer "falls through" the IF...THEN statement; falling through means that the next numbered statement is executed. The symbols for comparisons in the IF part are as follows: > is "greater than," > = is "greater than or equal to," < is "less than," < = is "less than or equal to," and < > is "not equal to." Compound logical tests are usually allowed, using OR and AND connectives. The action after the THEN can be any one of several valid BASIC statements, but some possibilities are usually not allowed (such as DATA, another IF...THEN, or a FOR...NEXT). Some examples are:

IF A = 0 THEN A = 1	If the current value of A is 0, then the computer assigns the value of 1 to A.
IF A = 0 OR B$ < > "HELP" THEN PRINT D ↑ 2, B$	If A = 0 or if B$ is any string other than HELP, D² and B$ are printed.
IF J = 5 AND K > = 3.47 THEN GOTO 50	If the current value of J is 5 and the current value of K is greater than or equal to 3.47 control is passed to statement 50. If J is not 5 or K is less than 3.47 the GOTO is not executed.

When mixing ORs and ANDs, be careful of the order in which the expression is evaluated—usually ORs first and then ANDs. Parentheses can be used to force any order desired.

Various forms of the THEN GOTO are often allowed. Test your BASIC to see if the following are equivalent:

IF A = 0 THEN GOTO 50
IF A = 0 GOTO 50
IF A = 0 THEN 50

With the GOTO, IF...THEN, and previously learned statements, you can program any loop. In fact, these statements allow you to write almost any program that does not need access to mass storage (disks, tapes, and the like) and that does not use a lot of variables. Most of the remaining BASIC statements merely make programming more convenient. For example, the following program implements the previous flowchart:

```
10  C = 1
20  S = 0
30  S = S + C
40  C = C + 1
50  IF C < = 1000 GOTO 30
60  PRINT S
70  END
```

Have the class program the example flowchart in Fig. 4-1 that determines which of two numbers is closest to a third number. (Note that ABS (X) gives the absolute value of X.)

```
 10  INPUT A,X,Y
 20  IF A = 0 GOTO 130
 30  D1 = ABS (A - X)
 40  D2 = ABS (A - Y)
 50  IF D1 = D2 GOTO 90
 60  IF D1 > D2 GOTO 110
 70  PRINT X
 80  GOTO 10
 90  PRINT X,Y
100  GOTO 10
110  PRINT Y
120  GOTO 10
130  END
```

3. *FOR...NEXT* statements automate parts 1, 3, 4, and 5 of the loop requirements. Unlike IF...THEN, which is one statement, FOR...NEXT is two statements—a FOR statement and a NEXT statement. The format and example of a FOR statement are:

Format: FOR numeric variable = expression 1 TO expression 2 STEP expression 3

   Example: FOR I = 1 TO 10 STEP 2

For the NEXT statement they are:

Format: NEXT numeric variable.
   Example: NEXT I

Note that the numeric variable in the two statements must be the same. Even if your BASIC doesn't require any mention of the numeric variable in the NEXT statement (that is, if you can say NEXT rather than NEXT I), mentioning the variable is so helpful from a documentation standpoint (so that you know which NEXT belongs to which FOR) that its use should be considered mandatory.

The positions of the FOR and NEXT statements define the top and bottom of the loop performed. Before the first pass through the code between the FOR and NEXT, the numeric variable is set equal to the value of expression 1. Each time the NEXT is encountered the value of expression 3 is added to the numeric variable. If the new value of the numeric variable is still between expression 1 and expression 2, then the loop is again executed starting with the statement after the FOR statement. But if the value of the numeric variable is no longer between expressions 1 and 2, then the execution of the loop is terminated, and the statement after the NEXT is executed. Note therefore that at least one pass through a loop is executed no matter what the values of the three expressions are.

Finally, note that the "STEP expression 3" is optional, and it is assumed to be STEP 1 if omitted. For example:

FOR Statement	Number of Times Loop is Executed
FOR I = 1 TO 10	10
FOR I = 1 TO 10 STEP 1	10
FOR I = 1 TO 10 STEP − 1	1
FOR X = 5.37 TO − 11.49 STEP − 1.45	12
FOR M = V + 5 TO Z (X + 5) STEP T − 2	—

Now going back to the program (Fig. 4-2) to find the sum of all integers between 1 and 1,000, again note how the FOR...NEXT combination performs parts 1, 3, 4, and 5 of loop processing:

```
10  S = 0
20  FOR C = 1 TO 1000
30  S = S + C
40  NEXT C
50  PRINT S
60  END
```

However, the program shown in Fig. 4-1, whose loop was implemented with an IF...THEN, does not lend itself to the use of a FOR...NEXT, since there is no predetermined limit on the number of times the loop should be executed—it is terminated by a particular operator input.

As a final note, FOR...NEXT loops can be *nested*, that is, placed completely within each other. There is usually no practical limit to the level of nesting. To print the product of each possible combination of two numbers between 1 and 10, the program is:

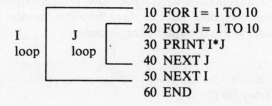

```
            10  FOR I = 1 TO 10
            20  FOR J = 1 TO 10
I      J    30  PRINT I*J
loop   loop 40  NEXT J
            50  NEXT I
            60  END
```

Week Four

Session 1. The next two statements, READ and DATA, come paired. Their formats are:

READ V_1, V_2,...V_n
DATA D_1, D_2,...D_n

Each V_i is a variable name—string or numeric. Each D_i is a string or number that is assigned to a particular variable name by a READ statement. (Particular rules for quotes around strings depend on your BASIC.) Note that it is not the number of statements of each type that must match. Rather, the number of variables read by any number of READ statements must not be greater than the number of variable values in any number of DATA statements. DATA statements should be at the end of the program, just before the END statement. For example:

1. To read and print the sum of two numbers:

   ```
   10 READ A,B
   20 PRINT A + B
   30 GOTO 50
   40 DATA 5,8
   50 END
   ```

2. To read and print a given number of character strings:

   ```
   10  READ N
   20  FOR I = 1 TO N
   30  READ A$
   40  PRINT A$
   50  NEXT I
   60  GOTO 999
   70  DATA 5, ABC, DEF, HELLO
   80  DATA PHOOEY, "HEY YOU KID"
   999 END
   ```

Next, describe the functions SQR, ABS, SGN, INT, RND, and any others available on your computer. Each of these functions operates on an expression in parentheses and may be part of any expression:

```
X = SQR (A)*3
PRINT ABS (B + 6) - 3
FOR I = INT(M) TO 15
```

Each function is described below:

    1. *SQR* finds the square root of the expression in parentheses:

SQR(4) is 2
SQR(3*X + A) is 2.646 if X = 2 and A = 1

    2. *ABS* returns the absolute value of the expression:

ABS(4) is 4
ABS(− 4) is 4

    3. *SGN* returns a − 1 for a negative expression, a + 1 for a positive nonzero expression, and a 0 for an expression with a zero value.

    4. *INT* returns the greatest integer that is less than or equal to the expression. This operation is the same as dropping the fractional part of a positive expression; but for a negative expression, the fractional element is, in terms of the statement, equivalent to the next greater absolute value:

      INT (1) is 1
      INT (1.3) is 1
      INT (− 1) is − 1
      INT (− .2) is − 2

INT is used for such things as:

    a. testing to see if an input is an integer:

      10 INPUT A
      20 IF A < > INT (A) GO TO (*error routine*)

    b. testing to see if a number is even or odd:

      10 IF A = 2*INT (A/2) GOTO (*even routine*)
      20 (*odd routine starts here*)

    IF A = 3, then INT(A/2) will be 1; and the test will fail.

    c. limiting the number of fractional digits printed.
      BASIC prints as many nonzero fractional digits as the number

contains. To print at most one fractional digit of a number (positive or negative):

```
10  X = INT(X*10)/10
20  PRINT X
```

If X = 53.7956, then:

```
X*10 is 537.956
INT(X*10) is 537
INT(X*10)/10 is 53.7
```

Note that no rounding occurs. To round a positive or negative number, add .5:

```
10  X = INT(X*10 + .5)/10
```

To round and print at most two fractional digits:

```
10  X = INT(X*100 + .5)/100
```

5. *RND* returns a pseudo-random number X such that $0 \leq X < 1$. The meaning of the expression in parentheses differs from one BASIC to another, and it often controls the "randomness" of the result. Some BASICs allow the statement RANDOMIZE, which is put at the beginning of a program to get the pseudo-random number generator started at a "random" point. Other BASICs use RND(1) to do the same thing. The PET BASIC currently has a bug that defeats this intent, but the current time can be used as the argument to accomplish the same thing: RND(TI). This starting point is used in most of the programs in this book.

Note carefully that the number returned by RND is always less than 1. Thus, if X is greater than 0, the statement

```
R = RND(1)*X
```

yields a number R such that $0 \leq R < X - 1$. Thus, if X is an integer greater than 0, then the statement

```
R = INT (RND(1)*X)
```

yields an integer R such that $0 \leq R \quad X - 1$.

Consider a requirement to generate a pseudo-random integer between 10 and 99. Thus, there are to be 90 possible integers starting at 10:

$$R = INT(RND(1)*90) + 10$$

Session 2. Describe the DIM and MAT statements.

1. *DIM* (short for DIMENSION) defines a set of many variables as having the same basic name, differentiated by numbers in parentheses following the name. This set of variables is called an *array* or *matrix*. The format for the DIM statement is:

DIM variable name $(d_1, d_2, \ldots d_n)$

The variable name can be a numeric or string variable name. Each d_i must be non-negative, and n (the number of dimensions or subscripts) must be greater than 0. The number of variables so defined is $(d_1 + 1)*(d_2 + 1) \ldots *(d_n + 1)$. The first variable in an array named A is $A(0,0,0\ldots0)$, and the last variable is $A(d_1, d_2, \ldots d_n)$. For most applications, you have no need for more than two dimensions (as in a table of values with both columns and rows). In that case, the array is dimensioned as follows:

DIM A(X,Y) when X is the number of columns (or rows),
         and Y is the number of rows (or columns).

This set-up is called a *double-subscripted array*. A list of words, on the other hand, is put into a single-subscripted array, dimensioned as follows:

DIM I$(X) where X is the number of words in the list.

For example:

```
10 DIM A(5,3)
20 A(1,3) = 7.2
30 A(2,1) = 4.5
40 PRINT A(1,3)*A(2,1)
50 END
```

Or, to read the 10 values in a DATA statement into an array:

```
10 DIM A(2,5)
20 FOR I = 1 TO 2
30 FOR J = 1 TO 5
```

```
40  READ A(I,J)
50  NEXT J
60  NEXT I
70  GOTO 90
80  DATA 5,2,1,7,7,8,3,5, – 6,13.39
90  END
```

2. *MAT* (short for MATRIX) statements, available in some BASICs, automatically perform matrix reads (as in the previous example), prints, additions, and multiplications.

Next discuss debugging procedures, which vary from one BASIC to another. Common to all is the capability to temporarily add one or more statements to a program to print out one or more current variable values as the program executes. Most BASICs allow the use of one or more STOP statements in a program to stop execution at a critical point. Once stopped, the program's status can be inspected by printing the current value of one or more variables using PRINT statements without line numbers. Variable values can be changed using LET statements without line numbers. Then the execution of the program can be resumed by typing a command like CONT (for Continue). After a STOP, the program can be modified, but you may not be able to continue it. Debugging capabilities unique to your BASIC should be investigated and discussed with the vendor.

Finally, standards for program documentation should be discussed. We emphasize the need to train students to adequately document their programs: This requirement should be a part of every assignment. The usual method. for documenting a BASIC program is with REMark statements within the program, explaining what is being done at each major point and which values are stored in the variables. The REM statements serve as reminders to the computer's user but cause no execution; they appear only in the program listing. Examples:

```
10  REM PROGRAM NAME
20  REM CALCULATES SUM OF INTEGERS BETWEEN 1
    AND 1000
30  REM S IS USED TO ACCUMULATE THE SUM
```

Session 3. Discuss the use of subroutines, describing GOSUB and RETURN and explaining when subroutines should be used.

1. A *subroutine* is a set of code that is called (i.e., made to execute) from another place in the program and then returns to the place from which it was called. Subroutines are usually used when a set of code must be executed at more than one place in the program. That code is written once as a subroutine, and the two (or more) places where it is needed call it out for execution.

2. A *GOSUB* statement calls the subroutine, and a *RETURN* terminates it. A GOSUB statement is followed by a statement number, and it causes control to be passed to that statement number. When a RETURN statement is encountered, control returns to the statement following the GOSUB. To illustrate:

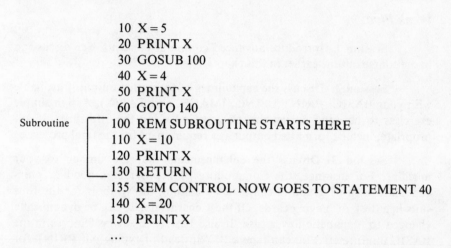

```
              10  X = 5
              20  PRINT X
              30  GOSUB 100
              40  X = 4
              50  PRINT X
              60  GOTO 140
Subroutine   ┌ 100  REM SUBROUTINE STARTS HERE
             │ 110  X = 10
             │ 120  PRINT X
             └ 130  RETURN
              135  REM CONTROL NOW GOES TO STATEMENT 40
              140  X = 20
              150  PRINT X
              ...
```

The printouts for this program are: 5, 10, 4, and 20.

Similar to FOR...NEXT loops, subroutines can be nested. However, whereas FOR...NEXT loops are physically nested, subroutines are not: Only their execution is nested:

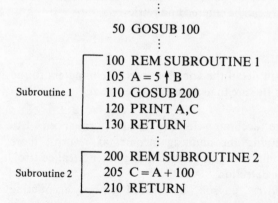

```
                    ⋮
              50  GOSUB 100
                    ⋮
                ┌ 100  REM SUBROUTINE 1
                │ 105  A = 5 ↑ B
Subroutine 1    │ 110  GOSUB 200
                │ 120  PRINT A,C
                └ 130  RETURN
                    ⋮
                ┌ 200  REM SUBROUTINE 2
Subroutine 2    │ 205  C = A + 100
                └ 210  RETURN
```

Subroutine 1 begins execution. Then subroutine 2 is called and completed before returning to subroutine 1 (line 120), which then also completes. Thus, the execution (*not* the code) of subroutine 2 is completely nested within the execution (not the code) of subroutine 1.

Stress the advantages of subroutines—they save time in entering the program from the keyboard, save memory space, and save debugging time—as well as the disadvantage—more execution time. Note that changes to the main program can be made without altering the subroutine, and vice versa.

Week Five

Session 1. Introduce advanced computer concepts. See discussion in the course outline earlier in this chapter.

Session 2. Discuss the capabilities of formatted output if available with your BASIC: PRINT USING, IMAGE, and TAB(X). Assign simple exercises to be done during this class period using these features. If appropriate, include formatted output as a requirement for the final project.

Session 3. Discuss the enhancements that are unique to your machine. For instance, the Commodore PET provides a good graphics capability with 63 graphics characters including the symbols for the four suits in a deck of playing cards. Of these characters, 26 can be dynamically changed to alphabetic lower case. It also has space saving features in the BASIC interpreter: You can type a "?" instead of typing out PRINT for PRINT statements, and you are allowed multiple statements (separated by a colon) on each line. The two instructions PEEK and POKE allow you to read specific memory locations (or other special locations, like the 1,000 CRT character positions) and put values into them, respectively. An instruction named GET retrieves only one character (if available) from the keyboard *without* a carriage return and leaves control of the cursor within the program. The time of day can be entered and retrieved.

Week Six

Session 1. Discuss in detail the contributions of computers to the various parts of our society. Be sure to include examples from:

1. *Government*: more accurate election returns, enhanced IRS procedures in verifying and auditing income tax returns, more accurate census tabulations and predictions, greater fiscal control, and improved crime detection,
2. *Business and industry:* payroll, automated general accounting procedures, tighter control of budgets, better predictions of business cycles and consumer demand, computer control of dangerous industrial processes, and inventory control, and
3. *Education:* student records, budget and accounting, registration and scheduling, instructional support, grade reporting, computer-assisted instruction, and demographic studies of historical events.

Session 2. Discuss some of the potential hazards of massive computer dependence in our society. First and foremost is the threat to privacy; data banks (large collections of data) that hold unnecessary information could be damaging to the individuals involved. Secondly, there is the possibility of computer fraud wherein the computer is used or even programmed to give preferential treatment to individuals or groups in such areas as the stock market, insurance, or any field involving privileged information. Thirdly, computer prediction of elections can have a considerable influence on the outcome of the elections. Then, of course, there is the inconvenience of incorrect bills that are difficult to have corrected. Finally, there is actually the danger of physical harm from an increasing dependence on computers: Think, for example, of the danger from a computer malfunction in the case of San Francisco's BART commuter system, where trains going in opposite directions use the same track based on computer-controlled scheduling!

At the end of the session, discuss with students how they can protect themselves from computer abuse—fighting back when a computerized bill is inaccurate, challenging erroneous information in data banks, providing minimum information on mass-consumed forms, and using similar tactics appropriately.

Session 3. Discuss the vocational implications of computers. In the last decade, computers have permeated many job fields, and this trend is bound to continue. Many students in the class will eventually work in jobs in which they interact at least occasionally with computers.

Describe common data processing and computer science careers, along with the training and education needed for them. Additional career information can be made available to interested students. (This information can probably be found in your vocational information data base, if you are lucky enough to have access to one.)

Week Seven

Session 1. Discuss computers and the future. Compare futuristic movies and literature with reality: Are the scenes from *1984*, *Star Wars*, and *2001: A Space Odyssey* that far away?

Describe the following as very possible scenarios in the foreseeable future:

1. All education is done at home, with students gathering only for supervised social interaction.
2. Home appliances are operated by computer on an "as needed" basis, eliminating the drudgery of today's housework.
3. Money disappears entirely from our economic system, and all funds are transferred electronically from the consumer to the manufacturer or the service bureau.

List of Problems

These require LET, PRINT, and INPUT:

1. Write a program to print the sum of 2081, 682, 1161, and 73.5.
2. Write a program to accept as input four numbers and print their sum.
3. Write a program that prints a decimal value for ⅔.
4. Write a program to print the product of two fractions that are to be input by the user.
5. Write a program to print the value of Y in the equation $Y = 2X^2 + 3X/5 + 12$ for a value of X that is to be input by the user.
6. Write a program to accept a temperature in degrees Fahrenheit and then to compute and print out the equivalent temperature in degrees Centigrade.
7. The speed of light is 2.99776×10^8 meters per second. Write a program to compute the speed of light in miles per second.
8. Write a program that multiplies two binomials. In other words, for $(AX + B)(CX + D)$, the user inputs A, B, C, and D; and the computer prints the expanded expression.
9. If a person begins saving money with 1 cent on a given day, doubles the amount he is saving the next day, doubles that again the next day, and so on for 30 days, how much money will the person have saved? Write a program to find the answer.
10. Write a program to determine the value of the change in the user's pocket. Have the computer ask for the number of each type of coin and then calculate the value.
11. Write a program that draws a picture of an object of your choice: the American flag, Snoopy, R2D2, whatever.

These problems require looping statements (GOTO, IF...THEN, and FOR...NEXT):

1. Compute and print out the sum of the numbers from 1 to 10.
2. Using a FOR...NEXT loop, flowchart and write a program to find the product of the first ten integers.
3. Write a program to find the product of the first ten integers using an IF...THEN statement instead of the FOR...NEXT loop.
4. Compute and print out the sum of the squares of the digits from N1 to N2, with N1 and N2 input by the user.
5. Flowchart and write a program to print the sum of all possible pairs of integers from 15 to 20.

6. Write a program that calculates and prints all possible batting orders for a baseball team of 9 players. Can you wait for it to end?

7. Flowchart and write a program to find the amount of interest earned by $100 deposited for one year in a savings account at 6 percent per year with interest compounded four times yearly. Do this with and without loops. Compare the results.

To do these problems, the student must know the READ and DATA statements and/or one of the SQR, ABS, SGN, INT, and RND functions:

1. Students in a class had scores of 87, 76, 88, 94, 68, 73, 99, 75, 79, 45, 66, 81, 72, 65, and 79 on a recent test. Flowchart and write a program to compute the average score.

2. Flowchart and write a program that accepts more than one set of test scores, finds the average for each set in turn, and prints each average before going on to read the next set.

3. Flowchart and write a program to print all sets of three integers between 1 and 20 that can be the sides and hypotenuse of a right triangle.

4. Flowchart and write a program to find the number of and the sum of all positive integers greater than 1,000 and less than 2,213 that are divisible by 11.

5. Write a program to generate and print random three-digit numbers, where no two digits are the same.

6. The number 142,857 has many remarkable features. Here is one of the least known: 142,857 squared equals 20,408,122,449—and 142,857 = 20,408 + 122,449. There are four three-digit numbers with a similar property: square the number, add the number formed by the last three digits of the square to the number formed by the remaining digits, and the original number appears. One of these is the trivial number 001; slightly less trivial is 999. Write a program to find the other two. What is the sum of these two numbers? (Be careful of round-off error when separating the two values of the squared number.)

These require dimensioned variables:

1. Write a program to read a set of data and then to print the set in increasing numerical order.

2. Write a program to read a set of data, sort it into numerical order, and print the difference between each pair of contiguous numbers.

For instance, if the set contains 8, 5, and 6, the printout will be 1 and 2.

3. Write a program to read a set of subjects, a set of verbs, and a set of direct objects, and then print sentences generated by randomly picking one part of speech from each of the three sets.

Computer Puzzles

These programs are not easy. You may wish to assign them as final project selections.

1. Write a program to simulate an elevator, capable of stopping at four floors. It is controlled by two buttons on the middle two floors (up and down), a single button (up or down) on the top and bottom floors, and a set of four buttons in the elevator itself corresponding to the four floors.

The elevator is controlled in such a way that the buttons within it take precedence over those on each of the floors. However, the elevator can be made to stop at a floor as a result of a request there, if the elevator is passing through that floor in the right direction or if there is no request from within the elevator itself. If there are no requests at all, the elevator goes to the first floor.

Requests for the elevator are queued (that is, stored in memory) in their order of occurrence and, apart from the rules given above, are dealt with on a first-come-first-served basis.

The program simulating the elevator allows the user to press any of the buttons (by typing at the keyboard) after it arrives at a floor, whether or not it stopped there. Output from the program should indicate where the elevator is, the direction in which it is moving, and whether it is stopping on that floor. Input consists of any number of lines, each line containing a request from a floor (indicated by a floor number and a direction) or a request from the elevator (indicated by a floor number only).

2. 1,000 coins are tossed into the air. Those that fall tails are removed, and the remainder are tossed again. Those that are tails are removed—and so on. Of course, this is a tedious experiment to perform by hand but an easy one to simulate on the computer. Write a program to record the result of each tossing as a point on a graph with the "coins remaining" axis running across the screen and the "throw number" axis up and down the screen.

Changing the probability from fifty-fifty to an input value of X, the program written for this problem reflects radioactive decay. The program can be improved by allowing any decayed atoms to decay again as a second radioactive material with the same or different probability value. Output is then to consist of a graph of combined decay curves showing the number of atoms of each material as a function of time. Expand the program to include these enhancements.

3. Five men and a monkey are shipwrecked on a desert island. The men all gather coconuts the first day for food and pile them all together before going to sleep, with the understanding that the coconuts will be divided five ways the next morning. During the night, one man awakens and decides he doesn't trust the others. So he divides the pile into five equal piles with one coconut left over, which he gives to the monkey to keep it quiet. He hides his pile, puts the other four piles back together, and goes back to bed. During the night, each of the other four men repeats the same procedure; and each time the remaining pile divides evenly except for one extra, which goes to the monkey. In the morning, each man notices the pile is smaller than it was before bedtime but keeps quiet in the belief that he is the guilty party. The remaining pile is then divided into five equal parts— and the monkey squawks for not getting a coconut.

Write a program to determine the smallest number of coconuts that could have been in the original pile. How does this compare with $5^5 - 4$? Have the program calculate several more answers to the problem. What is the spacing between answers? Why? Change the program to handle seven men. How does the answer compare to $7^7 - 6$? Does the formula work for an even number of men?

Note that the analysis of this problem is much more difficult than the programming.

4. A magic square is a square array of numbers such that the sum of each row, column, and diagonal is the same. An example of such a square, whose sum in all directions is 15, follows:

8	1	6
3	5	7
4	9	2

In the following square, "a" through "i" mark the spaces of the magic square, while "aa" through "ee" mark spaces outside the square.

	aa	bb	cc
a	b	c	dd
d	e	f	ee
g	h	i	

A set of rules for generating an odd (3 × 3, 5 × 5, and so on) magic square is:

a. Start in the middle top space (location b) with a 1.

b. The next higher number goes into the space that is up and to the right from the last number, if that space is in the square and empty.

c. If rule b takes you out of the upper right-hand corner (to cc), then the next higher number goes to the space below the last number (f).

d. If rule b takes you to any other column above the first row (aa or bb), then the next number goes in the bottom of the corresponding column (h or i).

e. If rule b takes you to any other row to the right of the right-hand column of the square (dd or ee), the next number goes to the left-hand side of that row (a or d).

f. If rule b takes you to an occupied space (for example b), then the next number goes below the previous number (g).

Write a program to calculate and print any odd magic square that fits on your printing device.

5. "Insanity cubes" are four cubes, each of which has one of four colors on each of its six faces. The object is to arrange the cubes in a row such that each of the four long sides of the resulting rectangular configuration shows all four colors on the four exposed faces. Write a program that accepts a specification of the color on each face of each cube and that prints the answer (if any). (Note that you need some consistent scheme for identifying the orientation of each cube; for example, if face 1 is up, then face 2 is down, face 3 is on the left, and so on.)

Notes on Building a Computer from a Kit

We have a few suggestions for those teachers brave enough to build their own computers as a class project. First, buy an inexpensive kit so you needn't be nervous with students working on it. Second, review the documentation *before* you buy; and if possible talk to someone who has already built one. In some cases, the documentation bears little resemblance to the task to be accomplished; and in others the how-to-do-it instructions consist of a single page that combine parts lists with "global" instructions—in other words, "assemble it."

Building a computer from a kit can nonetheless be a very valuable learning experience for students. During a project of this kind they develop skills in constructing digital components, learn how to read and work from circuit diagrams and schematics, and gain some experience in mechanical skills such as wire-stripping and soldering.

You should have some soldering experience yourself before you begin the project, and you will need a basic tool kit (a simple but adequate one can be obtained from electronics stores, such as Radio Shack, for about

$10). The class, too, should practice a little before beginning actual work on the kit.

Once you begin construction from the kit, we suggest that students work in groups of three or four, each group on a different task, with other groups checking the work that has been done. You should *plan* for assembly bugs—they are going to be there and you need a plan for troubleshooting them. One suggestion is to establish a good relationship with a manufacturer's representative (preferably someone at the factory) that you can call when you run into a stone wall.

If building a one-board kit merely whets the appetite of your students, then move on to the construction of a complete computer system. In one semester with advanced students, you can expect to build a complete computer system, including a computer, memory, TV terminal interface, and tape cassette interface.

Suggested Topics for an Advanced Computer Course

Although we don't have the space for a full course syllabus for a more advanced programming class, we do have space for a list of suggested topics:

1. memory organization (bits, bytes, words, and the like)
2. binary, octal, and hexadecimal representation and arithmetic
3. a. data types (integer, floating point, string)
   b. size of each type (use free core interrogative capability)
   c. representation of each type
4. floating point problems (comparison to 0, and FOR...NEXT loops)
5. arrays (multiple dimensions, storage, addressing)
6. lists and rings
7. sorting and searching
8. assemblers, compilers, and interpreters
9. files
10. numerical analysis (equation solving, such as square roots, and integration, such as pi)

References

Albrecht, Bob, *et al., BASIC*; 2nd ed. New York: John Wiley & Sons, Inc., 1978.
_____ , *My Computer Likes Me When I Speak BASIC*. Menlo Park, Cal.: Dymax, 1972.
Coan, James S., *Basic BASIC*. Rochelle Park, N.J.: Hayden Book Co., Inc., 1970.
Conference Board of the Mathematical Sciences, Committee on Education, *Recommendations Regarding Computers in High School Education*, 1972.
Danver, Jean, *Suggestions for Programs*. Hanover, N.H., Kiewit Computation Center, 1970.

Dwyer, Thomas, *A Guided Tour of Computer Programming in BASIC*. New York: Houghton-Mifflin Company, 1973.

Gateley, Wilson Y. and Gary G. Bitter, *BASIC for Beginners*. New York: McGraw-Hill, Inc., 1970.

Gray, Stephen Barrat, "34 Books on BASIC," *Creative Computing* (serialized beginning March 1975).

Introduction to an Algorithmic Language (BASIC). National Council of Teachers of Mathematics, 1972.

Rosenblatt, Lisa and Judah Rosenblatt, *Simplified BASIC Programming: With Companion Problems*. Reading, Mass.: Addison-Wesley Publishing Company, Inc., 1973.

Simon, David E., *BASIC from the Ground Up*. Rochelle Park, N.J.: Hayden Book Co., Inc., 1978.

Smith, Mark and Norman Sondak, "Computer Science at the Secondary Level," *AEDS 1977 Proceedings*, Fort Worth, Tex.

Smith, Robert E., *Discovering BASIC*. Rochelle Park, N.J.: Hayden Book Co., Inc., 1969.

Spencer, Donald, *A Guide to BASIC Programming*. Reading, Mass.: Addison-Wesley Publishing Company, Inc., 1969.

CHAPTER FIVE

PROBLEM-SOLVING

Every person trained as an educator knows how important it is to develop problem-solving skills. Activities that develop these skills are valuable because they ready students for everyday life, because they train them to think logically, and because they encourage them to pursue their natural curiosity and apply their natural creativity.

Problem-solving is generally thought of as an activity contained within the mathematics curriculum or the physical sciences laboratories. Yet it can be beneficially applied to the social sciences and, ultimately, to life in the adult world. To be sure, such skills developed in high school and in college are most readily used by the technical person in our society. Yet there isn't a profession or trade that can't benefit from the ability to think a problem through rationally.

Using the computer to help solve problems is a natural extension of problem-solving activities -started in the upper elementary grades. The computer-aided solution of a problem necessitates a thorough analysis of the problem and a very careful choice of a sequence of steps to arrive at the solution, not to mention the global evaluation of results to see if they are reasonable. This analysis of the problem, coupled with the construction of a sequence of steps to solve it, is described as an *algorithmic* approach to the problem.

In one sense, the entire educational process (in school and out) is composed of problem-solving. From the kindergartner attempting to link symbols with the spoken language to the biology student trying to quantify environmental equilibrium, from the elementary student learning double-digit division to the high school senior exploring the concepts of trigonometry—these children are being asked to understand complex (at least for them) processes. They are being challenged to sort out ideas, analyze them, relate them to their prior experience, and in general to integrate them into their daily lives. Every mathematics program introduces word problems at the upper elementary level; but problem-solving escalates from the trivial to the viable level only as children progress through junior high into high school, where they confront challenging problems outside the mathematics class—in the sciences, in social studies, in business classes. At this level they have hopefully acquired the skills they need, and their minds have matured enough that they can apply common sense as a test of results and seek alternative solutions if needed.

At this point the computer can make a big impact on children's education. Using the computer, they can explore real life problems in all subjects that are beyond either paper-and-pencil calculations or intuitive ability. They can study topics in mathematics that formerly weren't attempted because of the rigorous calculations required. They can study history and sociology from a demographic and statistical viewpoint. They can perform precise and detailed analyses of data collected from the chemistry or physics laboratory. And they can learn to evaluate the stock market, the commodities market, and other investment schemes in the business class.

With a computer, students learn more than ever before about the subject matter. They not only learn to solve problems relevant to future study and/or everyday life, but they also actually sharpen and refine their thinking ability in the process.

Over the last ten years, Project SOLO, conducted jointly by the Pittsburgh Public Schools and the Department of Computer Science at the University of Pittsburgh and supported in part by the National Science Foundation, has investigated just this type of creative use of computers in the secondary schools. The project, whose name was derived from the dual/solo sequence used in flight instruction, is a similar learning situation that develops advanced cognitive skills for students of tremendously varied backgrounds. The analogy between flight instruction and students using computers in their classes is quite appropriate. Emphasis in this project was placed on the solo mode, because of the power of the affective learning elements elicited when technology is used *by* students, not *on* them.*

We will show you some specific examples of the "solo" problem-solving approach, using the PET, and discuss how these examples are more a *supplement* than a *substitute* to regular classroom learning.

Where Calculators Fit

Electronic calculating machines can be easily and effectively used in any secondary math or science classroom. The handheld calculator is fast becoming as standard a tool for the math and science student as the slide rule or compass once was. A calculator can be used for the routine and often tedious calculations needed to explore higher-level concepts, to solve

---

*A good many curriculum units called *modules* were developed to support this approach for mathematics, physics, chemistry, biology, social science, and computer science. These modules are available for use in other schools.

problems that have previously been too time-consuming to be done with paper and pencil, and to serve as a flexible "answer key" to verify the results of hand computations. In addition, it can encourage students to be inquisitive and creative as they experiment with mathematical and scientific ideas; it can also help students formulate generalizations from displayed patterns of numbers and be a resource tool that promotes sudden independence in problem-solving.

A *programmable calculator* can be "programmed" with a set of instructions so that it can perform the same series of calculations time after time with the user inputting only new data each time. For instance, you could program a calculator to add two numbers, divide by 3, and take the square root of that value. It would do those steps in sequence whenever you input the two starting numbers until you cleared those program steps from its memory.

Computers are even more powerful. As we said in Chapter 4, we arbitrarily define three differences between calculators and computers (though there are exceptions, and the boundary is very hazy):

1. *Memory size and expandability:* Computers have more to start with and can be expanded.
2. *Speed:* Computers are at least ten times as fast.
3. *Use of peripherals:* Computers can use any number of peripherals, whereas the most a programmable calculator can use is a small tape printing device—no disks, CRTs, large printers, and the like.

Some of the problems described in this chapter can be solved with a calculator, but others require the capabilities of a computer. We will attempt to show the difference between a calculator-type problem and a computer-type problem. We advocate the availability of both devices in the classroom: Use the simple and inexpensive calculator to solve formulas and carry out difficult calculations; use the computer to develop an algorithmic approach to complex problems. With the first, you can relieve the student of much of the drudgery of technical subjects, and with the second you can open the door to more interesting and often exciting phenomena that could previously be studied only by those with sophisticated mathematical skills.

A Mixture of Mathematical Marvels

The Quadratic Equation

The simplest math application is programming the computer to solve a particular formula. Usually, although this can be done adequately on the calculator, it is a good beginning assignment when introducing the microcomputer to the class.

Exercise 1. The quadratic equation can be easily solved on a calculator. For the lesson value, however, write a program to find the real value(s) of x, given a, b, and c for the equation $ax^2 + bx + c = 0$.
Program.

```
READY.
10  INPUT A,B,C
20  X1=(-B+SQR(B↑2-4*A*C))/(2*A)
30  X2=(-B-SQR(B↑2-4*A*C))/(2*A)
40  PRINT X1,X2
50  GOTO 10
60  END
READY.
```

Both the computer and the calculator give some type of error indication if the roots are complex. To add a little variety, ask the students to write a program to calculate all values of x (real and complex) that make $ax^2 + bx + c = 0$ true, for a given a, b, and c.

Other Equations and Functions

Using a computer, students can investigate and solve polynomials of a higher order than quadratic equations, equations that would otherwise require higher-level mathematics to solve.

Exercise 2. Write a program to evaluate the polynomial $6x^4 + 2x^3 - 10x^2 - 6 = y$, for x = a to b in increments of s, with a, b, and s specified by the user.
Program.

```
READY.
10  REM****POLYNOMIAL EVALUATION****
20  PRINT "INPUT THE INTERVAL OVER WHICH"
30  PRINT"THE POLYNOMIAL IS TO BE EVALUATED,"
35  PRINT"AND THE INCREMENT TO BE USED."
36  PRINT
40  PRINT"E.G., TO EVALUATE OVER THE INTERVAL "
41  PRINT"FROM X=1 TO X=3, INCREMENTING BY .01"
42  PRINT"INPUT 1,3,.01"
45  PRINT
50  INPUT A,B,S
60  FOR X=A TO B STEP S
70  Y=6*X↑4+2*X↑3-10*X↑2-6
80  PRINT "X=";X;"Y=";Y
90  IF Y=0 THEN PRINT X;" IS A ZERO OF THE POLYNOMIAL."
100 NEXT X
110 END
READY.
```

Using this simple approach, also possible on many calculators, students can graph the function represented by that equation. The intervals surrounding the zeros of the function are evident, and the input can be modified to find the exact solution as far as the precision of the machine allows. This modification actually means narrowing the range between a and b, while reducing the size of s.

Greatest Common Divisor

One technique that is helpful is solving certain kinds of arithmetical exercises is finding the greatest common divisor for a set of integers. The simplest method, quite amenable to computer implementation, is educated guesswork.

Exercise 3(a). Write a program to find the greatest common divisor of a given set of positive integers. If the elements of the set are relatively prime, have the computer so indicate.
Program.

```
READY.
10 REM***GREATEST COMMON DIVISOR***
20 REM***TRIAL-AND-ERROR METHOD***
30 INPUT K
40 FOR I=1 TO K
50 READ N(I)
60 NEXT I
70 FOR D=1 TO N(1)
80 FOR I=1 TO K
90 IF N(I)/D<>INT(N(I)/D) THEN 120
100 NEXT I
110 LET X=D
120 NEXT D
130 IF X=1 THEN 160
140 PRINT "GREATEST COMMON DIVISOR IS";
145 PRINT X
150 GOTO 180
160 PRINT "SET OF INTEGERS IS RELATIVELY PRIME"
170 DATA 39,26,182,286
180 END
READY.
```

A more efficient method for finding the greatest common divisor is the *Euclidean Algorithm*. This algorithm modifies the division algorithm; that is, for any integers a and b, there exist integers q and r such that $a = b(q) + r$. The Euclidean Algorithm takes two integers of the set and assigns them to a and b, assigns q the value of the greatest integer for which $b(q) < a$, and finds the value of r. The integer a is then replaced with b and b with r, and the procedure is repeated until $r = 0$. The final value of b gives us the greatest common divisor of the integers a and b.

Exercise 3(b). Write a program that uses the Euclidean Algorithm to find the greatest common divisor for a given set of positive integers.

Program.

```
READY.

1 REM***EUCLIDEAN ALGORITHM***
10 READ K,A,B
20 C=2
30 Q=INT(A/B)
40 R=A-Q*B
50 IF R=1THEN 160
60 IF R=0 THEN 100
70 A=B
80 B=R
90 GOTO 30
100 IF C=K THEN 140
105 C=C+1
110 A=B
120 READ B
130 GOTO 30
140 PRINT "GREATEST COMMON DIVISOR IS";
145 PRINT B
150 GOTO 170
160 PRINT"GIVEN INTEGERS ARE RELATIVELY PRIME"
165 DATA 4,91,26,169,286
170 END
READY.
310

READY.
```

Prime Numbers

Another interesting assignment is generating a list of prime numbers. The program isn't difficult once the algórithm is developed—but an efficient algorithm is quite complicated. The key point is that the divisors to try are always less than the square root of the integer being tested for primeness.

Exercise 4. Write a program to accept a natural number n, and generate a list of all prime numbers less than or equal to n.

Program.

```
READY.

10 INPUT N
20 IF N>1 GOTO 45
30 PRINT"THAT'S TOO EASY.  GIVE ME ANOTHER ONE"
40 GOTO 10
45 PRINT 2
50 FOR I=2 TO N
60 SI=SQR(I)+.01
70 FOR J=2 TO SI
80 Q=I/J
90 IF INT(Q)=Q GOTO 120
100 NEXT J
110 PRINT I
120 NEXT I
130 GOTO 10
140 END
READY.
```

Trigonometry

Most computers and many calculators have built-in trigonometric functions, enabling the solution of realistic problems. The following problem is solved with the sine or cosine function.

Exercise 5 (a). Jonathan has a 36-foot ladder that he is going to use to paint the second story trim of his house. The directions say that the angle formed by the top of the ladder and the side of the house should be between 14 and 15 degrees. How far should the ladder be from the house at the bottom? (Determine whether your computer works with degrees or radians: Division by 180 changes degrees to radians. The output of the following program is in degrees.)
Program.

```
10 D1=36*SIN(14*/180)
20 D2=36*SIN(15*/180)
30 PRINT"BETWEEN";D1;" AND";D2
40 END
READY.
```

Again, this kind of calculation can be done on a scientific calculator. But if you decide to vary the length of the ladder, the computer can do it all with one program.

Exercise 5(b). Modify your program so it computes the proper distance from the house for ladders varying from 20 to 40 feet.
Program.

```
10 S4=SIN(14*/180)
20 S5=SIN(15*/180)
30 FOR I=20 TO 40
40 PRINT"BETWEEN";I*S4;" AND";I*S5;" FOR A";I;" FT LADDER"
50 NEXT I
60 END
```

Everyday Life

Many times in adult life we are asked to evaluate and choose between various kinds of financial arrangements, such as mortgage payment schedules or other investment schemes. Special-purpose financial calculators can solve this kind of problem, but the computer does it faster and for a greater number of situations.

Exercise 6(a). You are buying a new house with a purchase price of $36,000. You have $5,000 that you can use as a down payment. Write a program to evaluate the monthly payments and the total cost over the length of the loan for different down payments, interest rates, and terms of the loan. Note that the formula for calculating the monthly payment on a loan is:

$$\frac{PMT = PV*MI}{1 - 1 + MI} - NM$$

where

      PMT   is the monthly payment
      PV   is the amount borrowed
      MI   is the monthly interest rate (yearly rate divided by 12)
      NM   is the number of months of the loan

Use the information in the following table as input data once your program is established.

Down Payment ($)	Rate of interest (%)	Length of Loan (Years)
1,800	9.5	30
3,600	8.75	25
3,600	9.0	30
5,000	8.5	25
5,000	8.75	30

Based on the results of your program, which set of conditions would you choose? What assumptions did you make in order to make that choice?

      Program

```
10 READ DP,YI,NY
20 PV=36000-DP
30 MI=YI/12/100
40 NM=NY*12
50 PMT=PV*MI/(1-(1+MI)↑(-NM))
60 PRINT PMT,NM*PMT
70 GOTO 10
80 END
90 DATA 1800,9.5,30
100 DATA 3600,8.75,25
110 DATA 3600,9,30
120 DATA 5000,8.5,25
130 DATA 5000,8.75,30
READY.
```

      Exercise 6(b). Suppose that you have $6,000 you can use for a down payment on a house and that the largest monthly payment (principal and interest) you can comfortably afford is $350. Use the schedule from Exercise 6(a) and assume two things: (1) that any excess down payment is invested at 6 percent with dividends computed, paid, and withdrawn monthly and added to the $350 available for the payments; and (2) that the down payments in the Exercise 6(a) schedule are minimums. Under which financing plan can you afford the most expensive house? Now suppose the return on the excess down payment is 9 percent instead of 6 percent. Now 12 percent. Which plan is best?

An advanced question is: At a 9 percent return, why don't the 9 percent mortgage plans work out the same, regardless of whether the minimum or maximum down payment is used? (Hint: What if the dividends and some of the principal are withdrawn each time until all has been used at the end of the loan period?) Note that the amount that can be borrowed (PV) is:

$$PV = \frac{PMT*[1-(1+MI)^{-NM}]}{MI}$$

```
10 MAX=6000
20 IP=.06/12
30 READ DP,YI,NY
40 MI=YI/12/100
50 NM=NY*12
60 REM FIRST,PUT THE MAX DOWN
70 P1=MAX+350*(1-(1+MI)↑(-NM))/MI
80 REM NOW,PUT THE MINIMUM DOWN
90 P2=DP+(350+(MAX-DP)*IP)*(1-(1+MI)↑(-NM))/MI
100 PRINT P1,P2
110 GOTO 30
120 END
130 DATA 1800,9.5,30
140 DATA 3600,8.75,25
150 DATA 3600,9,30
160 DATA 5000,8.5,25
170 DATA 5000,8.75,30
READY.
```

Spectacular Science

Computers can be an aid both to the hard sciences, such as physics and chemistry, and to the life sciences, such as biology and zoology. There is quite a bit of good curriculum material available in physics and a little in the other disciplines. For instance, Project SOLO* produced some excellent modules in physics and chemistry, and Hewlett-Packard** published six units in physics and two in environmental science.

*For Project SOLO modules, write Digital Equipment Corporation, Maynard, Mass.

**For Hewlett-Packard's materials, including five Project SOLO modules, write: The Scientific Press, The Stanford Barn, Palo Alto, California 94304.

The Metric System

After threatening for years, this country is actually making a serious effort to convert to the metric system. In an attempt to level out the transition, educators have received directives since 1970 to teach metrics in their classes. The difficulties are similar to those encountered in teaching a foreign language: There is no correlation to life outside that particular classroom and there is no opportunity or reason to practice. The computer, however, can be used as a delivery vehicle for tutorial material on the relationships between our present system and metrics. It can also be used in the calculator mode to compute the actual conversion figures.

Exercise 7. Write a program that converts feet to meters, inches to centimeters, pounds to kilograms, and quarts to liters.

Program.

```
READY.

 10 PRINT"ENTER A NUMBER, A COMMA, THEN THE UNITS OF THE NUMBER TO BE CONVERTED:
"
 20 PRINT"     F=FEET"
 30 PRINT"     I=INCHES"
 40 PRINT"     P=POUNDS"
 50 PRINT"     Q=QUARTS"
 60 INPUT N,U$
 70 IF U$="F" GOTO 130
 80 IF U$="I" GOTO 160
 90 IF U$="P" GOTO 190
100 IF U$="Q" GOTO 220
110 PRINT"ILLEGAL UNITS"
120 GOTO 60
130 O=N*12*2.54/100
140 PRINT N;" FEET=";O;" METERS"
150 GOTO 60
160 O=N*2.54
170 PRINT N;" INCHES=";O;" CENTIMETERS"
180 GOTO 60
190 O=N*.45359237
200 PRINT N;" POUNDS=";O;" KILOGRAMS"
210 GOTO 60
220 O=N*.94635295
230 PRINT N;" QUARTS=";O;" LITERS"
240 GOTO 60
250 END
READY.
```

Electricity and Magnetism

The computer can make a particularly rich contribution to the study of physics. Many of the great ideas of physics can barely be touched without calculus and other equally advanced branches of mathematics. Using the computer, you can treat these ideas quite comprehensively with a familiarity with algebra and a little bit of trigonometry.

For example, one unit of the Hewlett-Packard Computer Curriculum Series explores the basic concepts of electricity and magnetism.

In this unit, students write computer programs to investigate these concepts, unhampered by tedious mathematical calculations. Topics include vectors, Coulomb's Law, electric potential, magnetic fields, electromagnetic induction, and circuits. Each topic is discussed, with background information and required formulas given, and programming exercises are assigned that demonstrate the ideas presented. Exercise 8 is one example from the section on circuits.

Exercise 8. Write a program using $Q_{new} = Q_{old} + (V/R - Q_{old/RC}) \Delta t$ to compute and print out the charge on the capacitor versus time. Use $V = 10$, $R = 2$, and $C = 2$. Use a time step of $t = 0.05$. Assume that the initial charge on the capacitor is zero. Let your program keep repeating calculations until interrupted manually at the terminal. Stop the program when the charge has reached the equilibrium value. How much time was needed to reach equilibrium? Sketch the results.

Program.

```
READY.
    10 REM***CAPACITOR-RESISTOR CIRCUIT***
    20 READ Q,V,R,C,D
    30 T=0:K=10
    40 PRINT:PRINT"TIME";"CHARGE":PRINT
    50 IF K<10 THEN 80
    60 PRINT INT(T*100+.5)/100,Q
    70 K=0
    80 Q=Q+(V/R-Q/(R*C))*D
    90 T=T+D:K=K+1
   100 GOTO 50
   110 DATA 0,10,2,2,.05
   120 END
READY.
   217

READY.
```

This exercise not only supports the discussion of analyzing circuits, but it also graphically reinforces the concept of equilibrium. The next two exercises explore the effects of varying the resistance in the same problem and of setting the potential charge equal to zero. Analyzing the circuit using this looping technique is much more effective than being presented with a printed table of values or even interacting with a "canned" program that does the same thing. In order to write and document the program, the student has to carefully consider the formula, and the thrill of discovering the trend through individual analysis reinforces the concept being explored.

Molecular Weight

A simple problem-solving activity in chemistry is writing a program to calculate the molecular weight of various compounds. The program in Exercise 9 allows only compounds made up of combinations of sixteen

common elements, but a simple modification of the data statements allows
the program to include any element on the periodic table.

Exercise 9. Write a program that accepts as input compounds made
up of sixteen common elements (O, H, N, C, F, B, Cl, Na, Fe, Mg, K, P, S,
Ag, Zn, Ca) and calculates the molecular weight.

Program.

```
READY.

 5 REM***MOLECULAR WEIGHT OF COMPOUNDS**
 10 DIM S$(16),W(16)
 15 PRINT "IN ORDER TO CALCULATE THE MOLECULAR"
 20 PRINT "WEIGHT OF YOUR COMPOUND, I WILL ASK YOU"
 25 PRINT "FOR THE NUMBER OF ELEMENTS IN YOUR"
 30 PRINT "COMPOUND AND THEN THE SYMBOL AND"
 35 PRINT "QUANTITY OF EACH ELEMENT IN TURN.  FOR"
 40 PRINT "EXAMPLE WATER WOULD BE INPUT AS:"
 45 PRINT
 50 PRINT"    ELEMENT #1? H,2"
 55 PRINT"    ELEMENT #2? O,1"
 60 PRINT:PRINT
 65 READ NT
 70 FOR I=1 TO NT
 80 READ S$(I),W(I)
 90 NEXT I
100 INPUT "HOW MANY ELEMENTS IN YOUR COMPOUND";N
105 PRINT
110 WT=0
120 FOR I=1 TO N
125 PRINT "ELEMENT #";I;
130 INPUT E$,C
150 FOR J=1 TO 16
160 IF E$<>S$(J) THEN 180
170 WT=WT+W(J)*C
175 GOTO 190
180 NEXT J
185 PRINT"I DON'T RECOGNIZE ";E$;".  INPUT IT AGAIN":GOTO 125
190 NEXT I
195 PRINT
200 PRINT "THE MOLECULAR WEIGHT IS";WT
205 PRINT:PRINT
206 GOTO 100
209 DATA 16
210 DATA O,16,H,1,C,12,N,14,F,19
220 DATA B,10.8,P,31,S,32,K,39,CL,35.5
230 DATA MG,24,NA,23,FE,55.8,CA,40
240 DATA AG,107.9,ZN,65.4
250 END
READY.
```

Human and Other Types of Genetics

Genetic probability can also be studied in more depth with the aid
of a computer. Genetics is very difficult to study in the laboratory, but,
given enough supporting information, computer programs can be devised
that simulate the reproduction of a particular species either over a number
of generations or for a large number of offspring. A simple program that
studies the passing of eye color in humans is elicited from students in

Exercise 10, which should be preceded by a discussion of dominant and recessive traits, genotypes, and phenotypes. (In Chapter 6, on "Instructional Simulation," a more complicated program is described that investigates genetic pairing more thoroughly.)

Exercise 10. Write a program that accepts as input the genotype of each parent with regard to eye color (brown or blue) and the number of offspring and that outputs the genotype and phenotype of each offspring, along with the phenotype ratio of brown to blue. Allow the user to suppress the printout of genotypes and phenotypes if he or she wishes. Run the program for n = 4, 10, 50, 100, and 500—and for all possible parental combinations. How do your ratios for the different numbers of offspring compare to the ones presented in class?

Program.

```
READY.
    10 DIM M$(2),F$(2)
    20 PRINT"ENTER THE GENOTYPE OF EACH PARENT,"
    30 PRINT"NUMBER OF OFFSPRING, AND IF THE"
    40 PRINT"RESULTS OF EACH OFFSPRING ARE TO BE"
    50 PRINT"PRINTED (Y FOR YES OR N FOR NO)."
    60 PRINT
    70 PRINT"EXAMPLE:  BR,BL,BL,BL,100,Y"
    80 INPUT M$(1),M$(2),F$(1),F$(2),N,P$
    90 BL=0
   100 FOR I=1 TO N
   110 O1$=M$(INT(RND(1)*2+1))
   120 O2$=F$(INT(RND(1)*2+1))
   130 O3$="BR"
   140 IF O1$="BR" OR O2$="BR" GOTO 170
   150 BL=BL+1
   160 O3$="BL"
   170 IF P$="Y" THEN PRINT I,O1$;",";O2$,O3$
   180 NEXT I
   190 BR=N+BL
   200 PRINT
   210 PRINT"RATIO FOR";N;"OFFSPRING IS";BR;":";BL
   220 IF BL<2 GOTO 80
   230 R=INT(BR/BL*10+.5)/10
   240 PRINT"WHICH IS";R;":1"
   250 GOTO 80
READY.
```

An Argument for Program Documentation

In order for a program to be useful to others, it must be documented. Written documentation should describe the program name, how to access it, what the user is expected to input, and which information is printed as output. Further, annotation of the actual program listing is needed to describe to others how the program works, that is, the logic of the program. This part of the documentation is done preferably with REMARK statements within the listing itself, *especially when working on a CRT-only*

```
GCD-DOC

10 REM***GREATEST COMMON DIVISOR***
20 REM***TRIAL-AND-ERROR METHOD***
21 REM
25 REM**INPUT THE NUMBER OF INTEGERS IN THE SET
30 INPUT K
40 FOR I=1 TO K
45 REM**READ IN ARRAY N, WHICH IS THE SET OF INTEGERS
50 READ N(I)
60 NEXT I
65 REM**TEST INTEGERS FROM 1 TO THE FIRST INTEGER IN THE SET
70 FOR D=1 TO N(1)
80 FOR I=1 TO K
85 REM**IF D DIVIDES N WITH NO REMAINDER, CHECK THE NEXT ELEMENT
90 IF N(I)/D<>INT(N(I)/D) THEN 120
100 NEXT I
110 LET X=D
120 NEXT D
125 REM***IF NONE OF THE D VALUES DIVIDES ALL OF THE INTEGERS,THE
126 REM***SET IS RELATIVELY PRIME
130 IF X=1 THEN 160
135 REM**IF X DIVIDES ALL OF THE INTEGERS, THEN IT IS A G.C.D.
140 PRINT "GREATEST COMMON DIVISOR IS":
145 PRINT X
150 GOTO 180
160 PRINT "SET OF INTEGERS IS RELATIVELY PRIME"
170 DATA 39,26,182,286
180 END
READY
```

GCD Annotated Listing

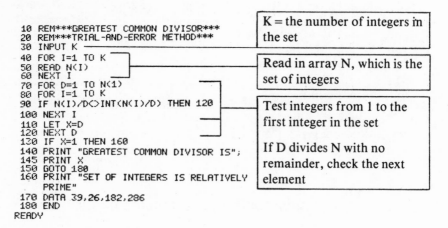

Fig. 5-1.

system; but when memory space is limited, comments can be written on a separate sheet or on a printout if one is available (see the examples in Fig. 5–1).

Such documentation is especially valuable to the teacher because it gives him or her insight into the cognitive processes used by the student in creating the program. A word of warning: *No* student or programmer voluntarily documents a program. Good documentation needs to be described, demonstrated, and then made a required part of any program submitted to satisfy an assignment.

Summing Up

The discussions and examples in this chapter should give you an indication of the tremendous contribution computers can make to a typical curriculum. The most common computer activity undertaken in the schools during 1975 was problem-solving in nature.* Experience suggests that students gain deeper insights into the subject when they write their own programs. When they are required to document them thoroughly, the instructor then gains insight into the depth of the student's understanding of the problem being solved. In other words, does the student know not only *how* to solve the problem but also *why* he or she did it that way?

Admittedly, the Hawthorne Effect proved true for many educational innovations, that is, the effectiveness palls when the novelty of the innovation wears off. But, to quote Thomas Dwyer, "Exactly the reverse has been true in the world of *real* computing."**

We advocate problem-solving on the computer not only because it is an effective way to study certain topics but also because students enjoy getting their teeth into real problems. Again quoting Dwyer, "The intrinsic fun of real computing should be preserved at all costs; it will translate into a joy for other learning given half a chance." That possibility alone is enough to justify making the means available to as many students as possible.

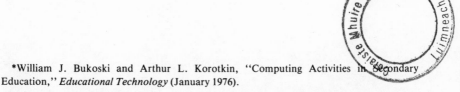

*William J. Bukoski and Arthur L. Korotkin, "Computing Activities in Secondary Education," *Educational Technology* (January 1976).

**Thomas A. Dwyer, "Teacher/Student-Authored CAI Using the NEWBASIC System," unpublished paper submitted to the Association for Computing Machinery, 1971.

References

Cratty, Bryant J., *Intelligence in Action*. Englewood Cliffs, N.J.: Prentice-Hall, Inc., 1973.

Davis, Gary A., *Psychology of Problem-Solving—Theory and Practice*. New York: Basic Books, Inc., 1973.

Houston Independent School District, *Computer Mathematics*, Curriculum Bulletin #74CBM6 (1972).

LaFave, L. J., G. D. Milbrandt, and D. W. Garth, *Problem-Solving/The Computer Approach*. New York: McGraw-Hill, Inc., 1972.

Polya, G., *How to Solve It, a New Aspect of Mathematical Method*, 2nd ed. Princeton, N.J.: Princeton University Press, 1957.

Sage, Edwin R., *Problem-Solving with the Computer*. Entelek, 1969.

San Diego City Schools, *Guide for Using the Computer in Geometry 1-2; Algebra 1-2; and Intermediate Algebra 1-2* (1966).

Spencer, Donald D., *Accent on BASIC*. Ormond Beach, Fla.: Camelot Publishing Co., 1977.

Spencer, Donald D., *Fun with Computers and BASIC*. Ormond Beach, Fla.: Camelot Publishing Co., 1976.

Spencer, Donald D., *Game Playing with BASIC*. Rochelle Park, N.J.: Hayden Book Co., Inc., 1977.

CHAPTER SIX

INSTRUCTIONAL SIMULATION

Instructional simulation is one of the most powerful applications of computers to education. This application involves the manipulation of a simplified situation that is analogous to the real situation you wish to study. Simulation enables the learner to make low risk decisions and receive harmless but informative feedback in the form of simulated consequences. With a simulation, the same event can be studied more than once, with the details slightly changed for variety if appropriate, allowing the learner to evolve more effective strategies over a series of attempts. The time frame of the simulated activity can be speeded up or slowed down to fit instructional goals. And, often without special provisions, an instructional simulation is entertaining and thus doubly motivating.

For instance, in a social or political simulation, the student is often put into a particular role and faced with the urgent problems and mandatory decisions inherent in that role; for a few minutes, he believes that the future *really* depends on him, a belief that will stimulate him to carefully consider the data and painstakingly examine the probable consequences of the various actions to take. Because he puts himself unreservedly into the event, he is more likely to internalize the concepts involved than with many other instructional approaches.

What Is a Computer Simulation?

There is not much agreement on the definition of simulations, especially regarding the similarities and differences between simulations and games. Some researchers even insert a third category, called simulation games. We call a *simulation* any computer model of a scientific or social event or phenomenon; purists would add restrictions pertaining to the formality of that model and would ask whether a competitive element is involved. We believe that entertaining activities can constitute the most effective instructional strategy and that the so-called "games" can therefore impart more understanding than the sometimes-less-interesting formal models of "reality." The simulations included in this chapter are a combination of straightforward simulation games and what are often called "serious" games. The next chapter contains examples of purely recreational games—"recreational" in that they are designed for no specific educational objective but still reinforce already acquired skills, often quite coincidentally.

Why Use Simulations?

Simulation enthusiasts—and we don't know many educators familiar with computers who don't fall into this category—can cite dozens of reasons for using simulations in the classroom. Some of these reasons are similar to those discussed in Chapter 2 for using computers in general: the opportunity to individualize instruction, the ability to motivate students who are indifferent to the educational process, the occasion to further stimulate already responsive students, and the chance to increase cognitive development through the use of the "discovery" method.

There are, however, unique reasons why computer simulations are a desirable addition to available classroom activities. First, simulations can be used to introduce a sense of realism into what are often frustratingly abstract subjects. Second, computer simulations involve the student in an active learning experience, removing him or her from the passive role of the traditional lecture class. Third, they often interest the student in the content of the subject by stimulating curiosity regarding cause and effect and by allowing reckless experimentation without any restrictions. Fourth—and tremendously important—they can be used as a stimulus to meaningful discussion. Often the debriefing session, during which students discuss their triumphs and failures and the teacher offers insights into the reasons behind their results, is the most valuable part of this activity. Last, since students often work in pairs or teams, the use of computer simulation leads to improved socialization among students who have not necessarily mastered the skills of cooperative "play." In other words, not only does the use of simulations expose students to a broader range of phenomena than before, it also enhances and intensifies their learning experiences while contributing to the development of social skills and team effort that will be needed in adult life.

The Right Place and the Right Time

As lavish as we have been with praise, we do insist on a word of warning: There is no *best* strategy that applies to all situations. Each situation should be evaluated for its needs, objectives should be developed, and *then and only then* should an instructional strategy be chosen that best meets those objectives. Sometimes this strategy is computer-based simulation; at other times an audio-visual presentation, a laboratory experiment, a reading assignment, or a traditional lecture is the appropriate technique.

Certain guidelines have been developed over a period of years concerning the appropriate times to use computer simulations. These guidelines were formulated in part during the course of two projects supported by the National Science Foundation: Huntington I and Huntington II, both under the direction of Dr. Lud Braun. (The Huntington projects are discussed in more detail later in the chapter.) In an article in early 1974,* Dr. Braun is quoted as having listed the following as objectives of simulation games:

1. to improve the student's understanding of subjects treated inadequately, if at all, in conventional laboratories;
2. to provide opportunities for learning by observation rather than vicariously by reading or by being lectured to;
3. to permit presentation in class of concepts not now possible because of limited student preparation in mathematics.

He goes on to delineate instances where simulations are appropriate as substitutes for real-life experiments:

1. when the experimental technique is complex and students are unlikely to be able to develop the needed skills (political prediction or biological and physical lab techniques);
2. when the time scale causes difficulty (genetic studies, population dynamics, economic and social predictions);
3. when certain danger is involved (radiation, heat, or corrosive, explosive or toxic substances);
4. when the exploration of systems governed by nonphysical laws is desirable (negative gravity, noninverse square gravitational systems).

In other words, computer simulation can be used to extend the boundaries of the traditional classroom or laboratory.

Clark Abt, in his classic reference work on gaming, states that self-directed learning in games occurs in three usually successive phases.

*"Huntington II Project Will Come to You," *Simulation/Gaming/News,* No. 11 (March 1974).

1. learning *facts* expressed in the game context and dynamics;
2. learning *processes* simulated by the game;
3. learning the relative costs and benefits, risks and potential rewards of alternative strategies of decision-making.*

Consider, for a moment, a game based on the actual occurrence of fourteen major battles of the Civil War. The sample run goes like this:

THIS IS A CIVIL WAR SIMULATION. TO PLAY,
TYPE A RESPONSE WHEN THE COMPUTER ASKS.
REMEMBER THAT ALL FACTORS ARE INTERRELATED
AND THAT YOUR RESPONSES COULD CHANGE HISTORY.
FACTS AND FIGURES USED ARE BASED ON THE ACTUAL
OCCURRENCE. MOST BATTLES TEND TO RESULT AS
THEY DID IN THE CIVIL WAR, BUT IT DEPENDS ON YOU.

THE OBJECT OF THE GAME IS TO WIN AS
MANY BATTLES AS POSSIBLE.

YOUR CHOICES FOR DEFENSIVE STRATEGY ARE:
(1) ARTILLERY ATTACK
(2) FORTIFICATION AGAINST FRONTAL ATTACK
(3) FORTIFICATION AGAINST FLANKING MANEUVERS
(4) FALLING BACK
YOUR CHOICES FOR OFFENSIVE STRATEGY ARE:
(1) ARTILLERY ATTACK
(2) FRONTAL ATTACK
(3) FLANKING MANEUVERS
(4) ENCIRCLEMENT
YOU MAY SURRENDER BY TYPING A '5' FOR YOUR
STRATEGY.

YOU ARE THE CONFEDERACY. GOOD LUCK!!!

THIS IS THE BATTLE OF BULL RUN (MANASSAS)
JULY 21, 1861. GEN. BEAUREGARD COMMANDING
THE SOUTH MET THE UNION FORCES WITH GEN.
MCDOWELL IN A PREMATURE BATTLE AT BULL
RUN. GEN JACKSON HELPED PUSH BACK THE
UNION ATTACK.

*Clark C. Abt, *Serious Games*. New York: The Viking Press, Inc., 1970. His definition of "serious games" is closer to the subject in this chapter than to the subject of games in the next chapter.

	CONFEDERACY	UNION
MEN	18000	18500
MONEY	$81000	$83300
INFLATION	25%	10%

HOW MUCH DO YOU WISH TO SPEND FOR FOOD? *4000*
HOW MUCH DO YOU WISH TO SPEND FOR SAL-
ARIES? *4000*
HOW MUCH DO YOU WISH TO SPEND FOR AM-
MUNITION? *73000*

MORALE IS POOR
YOU ARE ON THE DEFENSIVE

YOUR STRATEGY? *1*

	CONFEDERACY	UNION
CASUALTIES	2399	1887
DESERTIONS	82	6

YOUR CASUALTIES WERE 22% MORE THAN
THE ACTUAL CASUALTIES AT BULL RUN

YOU LOSE BULL RUN
- - - - - - - - - - - - -
THIS IS THE BATTLE OF SHILOH.
APRIL 6–7 ...

Using Abt's three phases, let's discuss some of the things students might
learn from playing this game:

1. Facts. Students playing this game absorb much of the factual
data concerning these decisive battles of the War between the States (dates,
names, generals, descriptions of situations, and the like). They notice the
wide disparity in inflation between North and South, and they make conjec-
tures concerning the effect of the troops.

2. Processes. Students learn that more decisions are to be made in
war than where to attack. They can experiment with different strategies and
decide how to apportion their money to achieve the greatest gain.

3. Relative Costs and Benefits. Playing this game, students begin to
understand the interrelated nature of factors in such complex processes as
war. The amount of money spent on food, salaries, and ammunition in-
fluences morale and the health of the troops: Spend too little on food, and

many soldiers become sick; spend too little on salaries, and poor morale causes desertions; spend too little on ammunition and casualties run high.

There Must Be a Catch

However, certain dangers and pitfalls are associated with the widespread use of computer simulations. For one thing, the students tend to think that because they understand the simple representation of the real life event, they also understand all the real phenomena similar to it. Thus if they understand a simulation of political campaigns in the 1928 election, they think they can fully evaluate influential factors in the 1976 election—when in truth radically different forces were at work in the two elections. Another problem is compensating for the inevitable bias of the designer of the simulation. This problem is minimal if the simulation is home-grown (unless it is difficult for the designer to admit his or her own bias); but, when the simulation is imported from somewhere else, the bias is not always identified in the accompanying documentation. Because simulation is such an absorbing activity, this type of bias has a potentially great impact on the student, and an attempt should be made to counteract it. Finally, the best simulation in the world won't be effective if it doesn't address your special needs. Careful evaluation, testing, and several rounds of modification are very often essential to the smooth usage of a particular simulation. However, if the limitations are carefully taken into account, the use of simulations in your classroom can be a broadening experience for you *and* your students.

Available Materials

The Huntington Projects

In 1968, the Huntington I project began with ten teachers from Huntington, Long Island. Their charter was to investigate computer education in the high schools. Subject matter specialists from nearby colleges were available as resource people to help identify topics that were amenable to computer study. Near the end of the second year, as funding grew to a close, a book of materials was published containing the eighty programs that had been developed in physics, chemistry, biology, earth science, and history. A proposal was then prepared for additional funding to pursue the study of computer simulation, since it had been found to be the most promising application developed in the preceding project. A grant was made, and the Huntington II Project was born. This project focused on biology and the social sciences, although a few simulations were done in physics and chemistry as a feasibility demonstration. Biology and social studies were chosen since the "captive" audience is large for both of these subjects—virtually all high school students are required to take them.

Each unit of the Huntington materials consists of three booklets:

1. The *student workbook* leads the student through a series of activities relating to the simulation. Relevant situations are described, and students are asked to use the simulation to evaluate their effects.
2. The *teacher's guide* describes the simulation, the rationale for using it, and the instructional goals. It also discusses preparatory activities for the class and provides a list of questions for follow-up classroom discussion.
3. The *resource handbook* provides extensive background reading, lists references, includes sample runs and a program listing, and thoroughly describes the mathematical model used to construct the simulation.

The Huntington materials can be obtained from Software Distribution Center, Digital Equipment Corporation, Maynard, Massachusetts 01754.

The next several pages contain discussions, sample runs, and listings of three of the Huntington simulations. The programs were modified for the PET but not to the extent of limiting the output so that only one CRT page is generated at any one time. This can be artificially accomplished by using the STOP key to look at a particular portion of the output, then typing CONT(return) to continue where you left off. One of the simulations produces output that needs to be viewed in its entirety; we include directions for modifying the listing to condense the output to fit a CRT screen. One last note: the listings are designed to direct output to the CRT; minor modifications were required (and are not shown) to list the output on a hard copy device. Consult your owner's manual for how to do this if you are using a printer with your computer.

Water Pollution (POLUT)
Subject: Biology; Grade Level: 10-12

POLUT simulates the interaction between water and two kinds of waste (industrial and sewage) in different environments. The student is allowed to vary certain factors and investigate their effect on the overall quality of a particular body of water. Here are the instructions given by the program if the student answers yes to the query "DO YOU WANT INSTRUCTIONS?"

IN THIS STUDY YOU CAN SPECIFY THE FOLLOWING CHARACTERISTICS:

A. THE KIND OF BODY OF WATER
    1. LARGE POND   3. SLOW RIVER
    2. LARGE LAKE   4. FAST RIVER

B. THE WATER TEMPERATURE IN DEGREES FAHRENHEIT

C. THE KIND OF WASTE DUMPED INTO THE WATER
    1. INDUSTRIAL
    2. SEWAGE

D. THE RATE OF DUMPING OF WASTE, IN PARTS PER MILLION (PPM)
    PER DAY.

E. THE TYPE OF TREATMENT OF THE WASTE:
    0. NONE
    1. PRIMARY (SEDIMENTATION OR PASSAGE THROUGH FINE SCREENS
        TO REMOVE GROSS SOLIDS)
    2. SECONDARY (SAND FILTERS OR THE ACTIVATED SLUDGE METHOD
        TO REMOVE DISSOLVED AND COLLOIDAL ORGANIC MATTER)

****

Next, the program asks for the value of the variables. The output below is based on the following input values:

> BODY OF WATER? *1*
> WATER TEMPERATURE? *50*
> KIND OF WASTE? *1*
> DUMPING RATE ? *8*
> TYPE OF TREATMENT? *0*

At this point, there is about a 60-second wait while the results are calculated, then the following message is printed: DO YOU WANT A TABLE, A GRAPH, OR BOTH? Both are shown below.

AFTER DAY 1 THE GAME FISH BEGIN TO DIE, BECAUSE THE OXYGEN
CONTENT OF THE WATER DROPPED BELOW 5 PPM.

TIME DAYS	OXY.CONTENT PPM	WASTE CONTENT PPM
0	6	2.67
1	5.24	9.82
2	3.41	15.38
3	1.16	19.69
4	0	23.04
5	0	25.64
6	0	27.66
7	0	29.23
8	0	30.44

9	0	31.39
10	0	32.12
11	0	32.69
12	0	33.13
13	0	33.48
14	0	33.74
15	0	33.95
16	0	34.11
17	0	34.23
18	0	34.33
19	0	34.41
20	0	34.46

```
              0.........5........10........15
                     (OXYGEN SCALE)
              0........20........40........60
                     (WASTE SCALE)
        DAY   |----|----|----|----|----|----|
         0    |W               O
         1    |      W        O
         2    |      OW
         3    | O          W
         4    0             W
         5    0                 W
         6    0                  W
         7    0                   W
         8    0                   W
         9    0                   W
        10    0                    W
        11    0                    W
        12    0                     W
        13    0                     W
        14    0                     W
        15    0                     W
        16    0                     W
        17    0                     W
        18    0                     W
        19    0                     W
        20    0                     W
```

Here is the listing:

```
READY.

 25 OPEN 4,4
 50 REM W1: WASTE FROM NATURAL POLLUTANTS INITIALIZATION
100 REM****POLUT--A HUNTINGTON TWO SIMULATION
105 REM     DEVELOPED AT THE POLYTECHNICINSTIIUTE OF BROOKLYN, 1971
106 REM     MODIFIED FOR THE COMMODORE  PET 8K MICROCOMPUTER, 1978
110 REM MAJOR VARIABLES:X=OXY. CONTENT;W1,W2,W=POLLUTION CONTENT

READY.

115 REM OTHERS DEFINED AS THEY APPEAR
135 DIM X(51),W(51)
140 PRINT"",,"WATER POLLUTION STUDY"
145 PRINT
150 PRINT:PRINT "INSTRUCTIONS (1=YES,0=NO)"
155 INPUT Q
160 IF Q=0 THEN 310
```

```
165 IF Q<>1 THEN 150
170 REM*** INTRODUCTION ***
185 PRINT:PRINT:PRINT"IN THIS STUDY YOU CAN SPECIFY ";
190 PRINT"THE FOLLOWING CHARACTERISTICS:":PRINT
200 PRINT"A. THE KIND OF BODY OF WATER:"
205 PRINT"    1. LARGE POND    3. SLOW RIVER"
210 PRINT"    2. LARGE LAKE    4. FAST RIVER
230 PRINT:PRINT"B. THE WATER TEMPERATURE IN DEGREES FAHRENHEIT"
240 PRINT:PRINT"C. THE KIND OF WASTE DUMPED INTO THE WATER:"
245 PRINT   "    1. INDUSTRIAL"
250 PRINT   "    2. SEWAGE"
260 PRINT:PRINT"D. THE RATE OF DUMPING OF WASTE, IN PARTS PER MILLION "
265 PRINT   "    (PPM) PER DAY."
275 PRINT:PRINT "E. THE TYPE OF TREATMENT OF THE WASTE:"
280 PRINT   "    0. NONE"
285 PRINT   "    1. PRIMARY (SEDIMENTATION OR PASSAGE THROUGH
290 PRINT   "       FINE SCREENS TO" REMOVE GROSS SOLIDS"
295 PRINT   "    2. SECONDARY (SAND FILTERS OR THE ACTIVATED SLUDGE METHOD
300 PRINT   "       TO" REMOVE DISSOLVED AND COLLOIDAL ORGANIC MATTER."
310 PRINT:PRINT:PRINT"***********************************"
330 REM*** INPUT PARAMETERS ***
335 INPUT "BODY OF WATER";Q
345 REM D1: RATE OF INJECTION OF NATURAL POLLUTANTS
350 D1=2
355 REM N: NATURAL WASTE DECOMPOSITION  COEFFICIENT
360 N=.75
365 REM C: RATE OF WATER ABSORPTION OF  OXYGEN (BASED ON Q)
370 IF Q=4 THEN C=3:GOTO 425
375 IF Q=3 THEN C=1.5:GOTO 425
380 IF Q=2 THEN C=1:GOTO 425
385 IF Q<>1 THEN 335
390 C=.4
425 INPUT "WATER TEMPERATURE";T
435 IF T>90 THEN 1055
440 IF T<=32 THEN 1070
445 IF T>50 THEN 465
450 REM X9:MAX OXY.CONTENT OF WATER
455 X9=15-2*(T-32)/9:GOTO 470
465 X9=11-(T-50)/9
470 INPUT "KIND OF WASTE";Q
480 REM H: HUMAN WASTE DECOMPOSITION CO-EFFICIENT
485 IF Q=2 THEN H=.75:GOTO 510
490 IF Q<>1 THEN 470
495 H=.25
510 INPUT "DUMPING RATE";D2
520 REM KEEPS D2 IN RANGE 0 TO 14
525 IF ABS(D2-7)>7 THEN 1040
535 REM W2:  WASTE DUE TO HUMANS: INITIALIZATION
540 REM X:  OXYGEN CONTENT: INITIALIZATION
545 W1=D1/N
550 W2=0
555 X=X9-D1/C
560 REM W(1),X(1) : INITIALIZE STORAGE ARRAYS (TOTAL WASTE,OXYGEN)
565 REM T2,K: STORE DAY FISH BEGIN TO DIE,IF THEY DO
570 REM T9: NEEDED FOR DAY COUNT,M:TOTAL DAYS FOR RUN
575 REM T1: INTEGRATION INTERVAL
580 T2=0
585 T9=0
590 K=0
595 T1=.1
600 W(1)=W1+W2
605 X(1)=X
610 M=31
615 REM D2: RATE OF INJECTION OF HUMAN  POLLUTANTS
620 INPUT "TYPE OF TREATMENT";Q
630 IF Q=0 THEN PRINT:PRINT:GOTO 670
635 IF Q=1 THEN D2=.5*D2:PRINT:GOTO 670
640 IF Q<>2 THEN 620
645 D2=.1*D2
670 FOR J=2 TO M
675 FOR I=1 TO 10
```

```
680 T9=T9+T1
685 REM PAIR OF DIFFERENTIAL EQUATIONS, EULER INTEGRATION
690 X=X+T1*(C*(X9-X)-N*W1-H*W2)
695 REM PREVENTS NEGATIVE OXYGEN LEVEL
700 IF X>0 THEN 710
705 X=0
710 W1=W1+T1*(D1-N*W1)
715 W2=W2+T1*(D2-H*W2)
720 IF X>5 THEN 740
725 K=K+1
730 IF K>1 THEN 740
735 T2=INT(T9)
740 NEXT I
745 REM W(J),X(J): STORAGE OF RESULTS IN ARRAYS
750 X(J)=X
755 W(J)=W1+W2
760 NEXT J
765 INPUT "DO YOU WANT A GRAPH(1), A TABLE(2),OR BOTH(3)";Q
775 IF (Q-1)*(Q-2)*(Q-3)<>0 THEN 765
780 PRINT:PRINT
790 REM*** TABLE OUTPUT ROUTINE ***
795 IF K<1 THEN 820
800 PRINT:PRINT
810 PRINT"AFTER DAY";T2;"THE GAME FISH BEGIN TO DIE, BECAUSE THE OXYGEN"
815 PRINT"CONTENT OF THE WATER DROPPED BELOW 5 PPM."
820 PRINT
825 IF Q<2 THEN 880
830 PRINT:PRINT
840 PRINT"TIME","OXY.CONTENT","WASTE CONTENT"
845 PRINT"DAYS","    PPM    ","    PPM    "
850 PRINT"----","-----------","-----------"
855 FOR J=1 TO M
860 PRINT J-1,INT(100*X(J)+.5)/100,,INT(100*W(J)+.5)/100
865 NEXT J
870 IF Q=2 THEN 1015
875 REM GRAPHING ROUTINE
880 PRINT:PRINT
890 PRINT"       0.........5.........10........15"
895 PRINT"            (OXYGEN SCALE)             "
900 PRINT"       0.......20........40........60"
905 PRINT"           (WASTE SCALE)              "
910 PRINT"DAY    I----I----I----I----I----I----I"
920 FOR J=1 TO M
925 PRINT J-1;TAB(5);"I";
930 IF 4*X(J)>W(J) THEN 945
935 PRINT TAB(6+INT(2*X(J)+.5));"O";TAB(6+INT(.5*W(J)+.5));"W"
940 GOTO 950
945 PRINT TAB(6+INT(.5*W(J)+.5));"W";TAB(6+INT(2*X(J)+.5));"O"
950 IF J<5 THEN 985
955 FOR K=1 TO 4
960 REM** DETERMINES WHEN SYSTEM HAS REACHED EQUILIBRIUM
965 IF INT(W(J)+.5)<> INT(W(J-5)+.5) THEN 985
970 IF INT(4*X(J)+.5)<>INT(4*X(J-K)+.5) THEN 985
975 NEXT K
980 GOTO 990
985 NEXT J
990 PRINT
995 PRINT"THE WASTE CONTENT AND OXYGEN CONTENT "
996 PRINT"WILL REMAIN AT THESE LEVELS UNTIL ONE"
1000 PRINT"OF THE VARIABLES CHANGES."
1015 PRINT:PRINT:INPUT"ANOTHER RUN(1=YES, 0=NO)";Q
1025 IF Q=1 THEN 310
1030 IF Q<>0 THEN 1015
1035 STOP
1040 PRINT"NEW YORK CITY ONLY POLLUTES ITS WATER"
1045 PRINT"AT THE RATE OF 12 PPM/DAY. MAKE YOUR"
1046 PRINT"RATE BETWEEN 0 AND 14."
1050 GOTO 510
1055 PRINT"THE WATER TEMPERATURE IS HIGH ENOUGH"
```

```
1056 PRINT"TO DESTROY MOST LIFE. TRY A NEW TEMPERATURE."
1065 GOTO 425
1070 PRINT"YOUR BODY OF WATER IS A BLOCK OF ICE"
1075 PRINT"AND CAN'T ACCEPT ANY WASTE. TRY A"
1076 PRINT"NEW TEMPERATURE."
1080 GOTO 425
1085 END
READY.
```

American Presidential Elections (ELECT 1,2)
Subject: Social Studies, Civics, History, Governments; Grade Level: 8-12

This simulation studies campaign strategy in fourteen past presidential elections, beginning with the election of 1828. The simulation is explained in the instructions printed below:

HISTORICAL ELECTIONS-19TH CENT.

YOUR GOAL WILL BE TO CHOOSE THE OPTIMUM STRATEGY
FOR CANDIDATES IN A HISTORICAL ELECTION.

EACH CANDIDATE'S STRATEGY CONSISTS OF 3 NUMBERS.
THE FIRST REPRESENTS THE AMOUNT OF EMPHASIS TO
BE PLACED ON THE CANDIDATE'S IMAGE.

THE SECOND REPRESENTS THE AMOUNT OF EMPHASIS TO
BE PLACED ON PARTY AFFILIATION.

THE THIRD REPRESENTS THE AMOUNT OF EMPHASIS TO
BE PLACED ON THE CAMPAIGN ISSUES.

EACH OF THESE NUMBERS IS BETWEEN 10 AND 80,
WITH A HIGHER NUMBER REPRESENTING MORE EMPHASIS.

THE TOTAL OF EACH STRATEGY MUST EQUAL 100!

THE COMPUTER WILL FIRST ASK THE ELECTION CODE NO.
CHOOSE THE CODE NO. FROM THE FOLLOWING LIST:

ELECTION	CODE NO.
1828	1
1840	2
1844	3
1868	4
1876	5
1884	6
1896	7

After choosing an election code, the student is told the two candidates and their party affiliations:

```
ELECTION OF 1828

CANDIDATE A                    CANDIDATE B
JACKSON                        ADAMS
DEMOCRAT                       NATIONAL REPUBLICAN
```

Then he inputs the strategy for each (as described in the instructions). The results of these strategies is then computed, and displayed along with the actual voting results from that election. The output below is based on identical strategies for both candidates: 30 (Image), 30 (Party), 40 (Issues).

```
THE RESULT OF YOUR STRATEGY IS:

JACKSON                        ADAMS
47%                            53%

THE VOTE FOR THE TWO MAJOR CANDIDATES
IN THE ACTUAL ELECTION:

JACKSON                        ADAMS
56%                            44%
```

Here is the listing:

```
READY.

10 REM***ELECT1 HUNTINGTON SIMULATION**
15 REM***  HISTORICAL ELECTIONS: 19TH    CENTURY
20 REM   DEVELOPED AT SUNY, 1972
25 REM   MODIFIED FOR COMMODORE PET 1978
60 DIM Y(8),W(9),M(72),I(3),S(3),P(16)
70 FOR I=1 TO 7
80 READ Y(I)
90 NEXT I
100 FOR I=1 TO 63
110 READ M(I)
120 NEXT I
130 FOR I=1 TO 14
140 READ P(I)
150 NEXT I
160 PRINT TAB(15);"ELECT1"
180 PRINT:PRINT TAB(8);"HISTORICAL ELECTIONS-19TH CENT."
190 PRINT
200 F=0
210 INPUT "WANT INSTRUCTIONS (1=YES,0=NO)";I
230 IF I=0 THEN 480
240 IF I<>1 THEN 210
250 PRINT:PRINT"YOUR GOAL WILL BE TO CHOOSE THE "
260 PRINT"OPTIMUM STRATEGY FOR CANDIDATES IN A"
270 PRINT"HISTORICAL ELECTION."
280 PRINT:PRINT"EACH CANDIDATE'S STRATEGY CONSISTS OF"
```

```
290 PRINT"3 NUMBERS. THE FIRST REPRESENTS THE "
300 PRINT"AMOUNT OF EMPHASIS TO BE PLACED ON"
310 PRINT"THE CANDIDATE'S IMAGE."
320 PRINT:PRINT"THE SECOND REPRESENTS THE AMOUNT OF"
330 PRINT"EMPHASIS TO BE PLACED ON PARTY AFFILIA-"
335 PRINT"TION."
350 PRINT:PRINT"THE THIRD REPRESENTS THE AMOUNT OF"
360 PRINT"EMPHASIS TO BE PLACED ON THE CAMPAIGN"
370 PRINT"ISSUES."
380 PRINT:PRINT"EACH OF THESE NUMBERS IS BETWEEN"
385 PRINT"10 AND 80, WITH A HIGHER NUMBER "
390 PRINT"REPRESENTING MORE EMPHASIS."
410 PRINT:PRINT"THE TOTAL OF EACH STRATEGY MUST"
420 PRINT"EQUAL 100!"
440 PRINT
450 PRINT"THE COMPUTER WILL FIRST ASK"
455 PRINT"THE ELECTION CODE NO."
456 PRINT "CHOOSE THE CODE NO. FROM THE"
460 PRINT"FOLLOWING LIST:"
470 GOTO 520
480 INPUT"DO YOU WANT CODE LIST (1=YES,0=NO)";I
500 IF I=0 THEN 570
510 IF I<>1 THEN 480
520 PRINT
530 PRINT:PRINT"       ELECTION",,"CODE NO. "
540 FOR I=1 TO 7
550 PRINT"          ";Y(I),,I
560 NEXT I
570 PRINT
580 PRINT"ELECTION CODE NO.";
590 INPUT E
600 FOR I=1 TO 7
610 IF I=E THEN 640
620 NEXT I
630 GOTO 456
640 X=(E*9)-8
650 PRINT
660 PRINT TAB(7);"ELECTION OF";Y(E)
670 PRINT
680 PRINT"     CANDIDATE A","CANDIDATE B"
690 IF E>1 THEN 720
700 PRINT"     JACKSON", "ADAMS"
710 GOTO 910
720 IF E>2 THEN 750
730 PRINT"     VAN BUREN  ","HARRISON"
740 GOTO 910
750 IF E>3 THEN 780
760 PRINT"    ' POLK",,"CLAY"
770 GOTO 910
780 IF E>4 THEN 810
790 PRINT"     SEYMOUR", "GRANT"
800 GOTO 910
810 IF E>5 THEN 840
820 PRINT"     TILDEN", "HAYES"
830 GOTO 910
840 IF E>6 THEN 870
850 PRINT"     CLEVELAND  ","BLAINE"
860 GOTO 910
870 PRINT"     MC KINLEY ","BRYAN"
880 IF F<>0 THEN 1230
890 PRINT"     REPUBLICAN";TAB(20);"DEMOCRAT"
900 GOTO 1000
910 IF F<>0 THEN 1230
920 PRINT"     DEMOCRAT";
930 IF E>1 THEN 960
940 PRINT TAB(20);"NATIONAL REPUBLICAN"
950 GOTO 1000
960 IF (E-2)*(E-3)=0 THEN 990
```

```
970 PRINT TAB(20);"REPUBLICAN"
980 GOTO 1000
990 PRINT TAB(20); "WHIG"
1000 PRINT
1010 PRINT"CANDIDATE A - ";
1020 GOSUB 1490
1030 S(1)=I(1)/100
1040 S(2)=I(2)/100
1050 S(3)=I(3)/100
1060 PRINT"CANDIDATE B - ";
1070 GOSUB 1490
1080 PRINT
1090 FOR J=1 TO 3
1100 W(J)=S(1)*M(X+J-1)
1110 NEXT J
1120 FOR J=4 TO 6
1130 W(J)=S(2)*M(X+J-1)
1140 NEXT J
1150 FOR J=7 TO 9
1160 W(J)=S(3)*M(X+J-1)
1170 NEXT J
1180 W(1)=W(1)+W(4)+W(7)
1190 W(2)=W(2)+W(5)+W(8)
1200 W(3)=W(3)+W(6)+W(9)
1210 A=W(1)*(I(1)/100)+W(2)*(I(2)/100)+W(3)*(I(3)/100)
1220 A1=((A-1)/4)*100
1230 IF F>0 THEN 1280
1240 PRINT"THE RESULT OF YOUR STRATEGY IS:"
1250 F=1
1260 PRINT
1270 GOTO 690
1280 IF F=2   THEN 1360
1290 PRINT"       ";A1;"%";TAB(20);100-A1;"%"
1300 PRINT
1310 PRINT"THE VOTE FOR THE TWO MAJOR CANDIDATES"
1320 PRINT"IN THE ACTUAL ELECTION:"
1330 F=2
1340 PRINT
1350 GOTO 690
1360 PRINT"       ";P(2*E-1);"%";TAB(20);P(2*E);"%"
1370 PRINT
1380 INPUT"ANOTHER RUN (1=YES,0=NO)";I
1400 IF I=1 THEN 190
1410 IF I<>0 THEN 1380
1420 GOTO 1600
1430 DATA 1828,1840,1844,1868,1876,1884      ,1896
1440 DATA 4,3,3,3,2,2,3,3,3,2,3,3,3,4,3,3,3,3,1,2,3,2,4,4,3,4,5
1450 DATA 1,3,3,3,4,3,3,3,2,2,3,2,3,3,3,3,4,4,3,3,3,3,2,2,3,2,3
1460 DATA 2,3,3,3,3,4,4,3,4,3
1470 DATA 56,44,47,53,50.7,49.3,47.3,52.7,51.5,48.5
1480 DATA 50.1,49.9,52.2,47.8
1490 PRINT"STRATEGY (3 NUMBERS,10<=I<=80,TOTAL=100)";
1500 INPUT I(1),I(2),I(3)
1510 FOR I=1 TO 3
1520 IF I(I)<10 THEN 1560
1530 NEXT I
1540 IF ABS(I(1)+I(2)+I(3)-100)>.01THEN      1580
1550 RETURN
1560 PRINT"EACH COMPONENT OF THE STRATEGY MUST BE"
1561 PRINT"AT LEAST 10!"
1570 GOTO 1490
1580 PRINT"THE TOTAL OF THE THREE NUMBERS MUST"
1581 PRINT"EQUAL 100!"
1590 GOTO 1490
1600 END
14602 ,3,3,3,4,4,3,4,3
READY.
```

Wave Theory of Light (SLITS)
Subject: Physics; Grade Level: 11-12

This program simulates Young's Double-Slit Experiment that demonstrates interference patterns for light. The student manipulates three variables, one at a time: the wavelength of the light source, the distance between the two slits, and the distance between the double-slit screen and the viewing screen. The computer then plots a graph of relative light intensity versus distance from the center of the viewing screen.

The output below shows the first part of a typical interaction with the program. First, an example is plotted to demonstrate the experiment.

```
        YOUNG'S DOUBLE SLIT EXPERIMENT


     L=2 METERS        W=6000 ANGSTROMS
     D=.5 MILLIMETERS

     Y AXIS IS DISTANCE (IN MM'S) FROM THE
     CENTER OF THE SCREEN
            -.26  ·                         *
            -.24  ·                          *
            -.22  ·                          *
            -.20  ·                    *
            -.18  ·               *
            -.16  ·          *
            -.14  · *
            -.12  *
            -.10  ·*
            -.08  · ·      *
            -.06  ·            *
            -.04  ·                 *
            -.02  ·                       *
     ....X AXIS IS LIGHT INTENSITY.......*...
             .02  ·                       *
             .04  ·                 *
             .06  ·           *
             .08  ·       *
             .10  ·*
             .12  *
             .14  · *
             .16  ·       *
             .18  ·            *
             .20  ·                 *
             .22  ·                    *
             .24  ·                      *
             .26  ·                      *
```

ABOVE IS AN ILLUSTRATIVE PLOT OF LIGHT INTENSITY ON
THE VIEWING SCREEN VERSUS DISTANCE FROM THE CENTER
OF THE SCREEN. THE PLOT USES PRE-DETERMINED VALUES
FOR WAVELENGTH (W), DISTANCE BETWEEN SLITS AND SCREEN (L),
AND CENTER-TO-CENTER SLIT SEPARATION (D). NOW YOU MAY
VARY THESE PARAMETERS, ONE AT A TIME.

****

WHAT IS THE NEW SLIT SEPARATION (D) IN MILLIMETERS?.7

(another plot will be generated using this new slit separation)

Then, at the computer's invitation, we changed the slit separation (D) from
.5 to 5 millimeters. The change in the plot of light intensity is quite
dramatic.

Now, we could continue to try different values for D, or go on to
one of the other two variables.

If you are using this simulation in a CRT-only environment, the
program should be changed to make the graph fit the screen, and to make
the program pause as long as the student wishes so she can study the
screen. To change the span of the graph, adjust lines 879 and 880 as shown;
to preserve the graph until any key is struck, make the modification to line
896.

> 879 A = − .2
> 880 B = .21
> 896 U = 0:GET A$:IF A$ = ""''GOTO896

The unmodified listing is shown below:

```
READY.

 50 REM SLITS--DEVELOPED BY HUNTINGTON II PROJECT-1971
 51 REM MODIFIED FOR COMMODORE PET-1978
100 REM YOUNG'S DOUBLE SLIT EXPERIMENT
103 REM IMPORTANT VARIABLES: L=DISTANCE FROM SLITS TO SCREEN;
       W=WAVELENGTH;
104 REM D=SLIT SEPARATION (CENTER TO CENTER)
105 REM
106 REM U=PRINT PARAMETER FOR UNKNOWN WAVELENGTH
107 U=0
110 PRINT "     YOUNG'S DOUBLE SLIT EXPERIMENT"
111 PRINT
120 REM ILLUSTRATIVE RUN
130 L=2
140 W=6000
150 D=.5
160 REM PLOT THIS COMBINATION
170 GOSUB 855
171 PRINT
172 PRINT "ABOVE IS AN ILLUSTRATIVE PLOT OF LIGHT"
173 PRINT "INTENSITY ON THE VIEWING SCREEN VERSUS"
174 PRINT "DISTANCE FROM THE CENTER OF THE SCREEN."
175 PRINT "THE PLOT USES PRE-DETERMINED VALUES FOR"
176 PRINT "WAVELENGTH (W), DISTANCE BETWEEN SLITS"
177 PRINT "AND SCREEN (L), AND CENTER-TO-CENTER"
178 PRINT "SLIT SEPARATION (D). NOW YOU MAY VARY"
179 PRINT "THESE PARAMETERS, ONE AT A TIME."
184 PRINT
185 PRINT "*****"
186 PRINT
190 REM CALL D INPUT SUBROUTINE
200 GOSUB 922
210 REM CALL PLOT ROUTINE
220 GOSUB 855
221 PRINT
230 PRINT "WOULD YOU LIKE TO TRY ANOTHER VALUE OF D(1=YES, 0=NO)";
240 INPUT Q1
250 IF Q1>0 THEN 200
260 PRINT
261 PRINT "*****"
262 PRINT
270 REM RESET D
```

```
280 D=.5
290 REM CALL W INPUT SUBROUTINE
300 GOSUB 944
310 REM CALL PLOT SUBROUTINE
320 GOSUB 855
321 PRINT
330 PRINT "WOULD YOU LIKE TO TRY ANOTHER VALUE OF W(1=YES, 0=NO)";
340 INPUT Q2
350 IF Q2>0 THEN 300
360 PRINT
361 PRINT "*****"
362 PRINT
370 REM RESET W
380 W=6000
390 REM CALL L INPUT SUBROUTINE
400 GOSUB 902
410 REM CALL PLOT SUBROUTINE
420 GOSUB 855
421 PRINT
430 PRINT "WOULD YOU LIKE TO TRY ANOTHER VALUE OF L(1=YES, 0=NO)";
440 INPUT Q3
450 IF Q3>0 THEN 400
460 PRINT
461 PRINT "*****"
462 PRINT
470 REM RESET L
480 L=2
490 PRINT "YOU WILL NOW BE GIVEN A LIGHT SOURCE OF"
491 PRINT "UNKNOWN WAVELENGTH.  YOU WILL SPECIFY"
492 PRINT "THE SLIT SEPARATION (D), AND THE"
493 PRINT "DISTANCE FROM SLITS TO SCREEN (L)."
507 REM Q5 DETERMINES IF W IS TO BE CHANGED
508 Q5=0
520 REM CALL D INPUT SUBROUTINE
530 GOSUB 922
550 REM CALL L INPUT SUBROUTINE
560 GOSUB 902
565 REM CHANGE W?
566 IF Q5>0 THEN 601
570 REM RANDOMLY DETERMINE WAVELENGTH
590 W=1000*INT(3*RND(TI)+4.5)
600 REM CALL PLOT SUBROUTINE WITH "UNKNOWN" W
601 U=1
605 GOSUB 855
606 PRINT
610 PRINT "WOULD YOU LIKE A PLOT FOR OTHER VALUES"
611 PRINT "OF D AND L (1=YES, 0=NO)";
620 INPUT Q5
630 IF Q5>0 THEN 530
640 PRINT "WHAT DO YOU THINK THE UNKNOWN WAVELENTH"
641 PRINT "(W) IS";
650 INPUT W1
660 IF ABS(W1-W)<.1*W THEN 700
670 PRINT "YOU ARE MORE THAN 10% OFF.  TO HELP,"
680 PRINT "YOU MAY OBTAIN MORE PLOTS."
690 GOTO 610
700 PRINT "GOOD!  THE WAVELENGTH WAS";W
701 PRINT "ANGSTROMS.  WOULD YOU LIKE TO TRY"
702 PRINT "ANOTHER UNKNOWN WAVELENGTH (1=YES,"
703 PRINT "0=NO)";
704 INPUT Q6
705 IF Q6<1 THEN 967
706 PRINT "YOU MAY SPECIFY A NEW SLIT SEPARATION"
707 PRINT "(D) AND DISTANCE FROM SLITS TO SCREEN"
708 PRINT "(L)."
709 GOTO 508
849 REM
850 REM PLOT ROUTINE
855 PRINT
```

```
856 PRINT
857 REM IF U>0 DO NOT PRINT WAVELENGTH
858 IF U>0 THEN 870
860 PRINT "L=";L;"METERS      W=";W;"ANGSTROMS"
865 GOTO 871
870 PRINT "L=";L;"METERS      W= ? ANGSTROMS"
871 PRINT "D=";D;"MILLIMETERS"
872 PRINT
875 PRINT "Y AXIS IS DISTANCE (IN MM'S) FROM THE"
876 PRINT "CENTER OF THE SCREEN"
877 REM A=LOWER LIMIT OF PLOT IN MM'S
878 REM B=UPPER LIMIT OF PLOT IN MM'S
879 A=-.26
880 B=.27
881 REM R=PRELIMINARY CALC FOR INTENSITY
882 REM 10E4 IS A CONVERSION FACTOR
884 R=(3.1416*D*10E4)/(W*L)
885 REM LOOP TO CALCULATE AND PLOT PATTERN
886 FOR X=A TO B STEP .02
887 REM Y=INTENSITY;  20=SCALE FACTOR FOR PLOT;  X=DISTANCE (MM'S)
888 Y=20*COS(R*X)*COS(R*X)
889 IF ABS(X)<.0001 THEN 894
890 PRINT TAB(8);INT(X*100+.5)/100;TAB(15);
891 IF Y>=.5 THEN PRINT ".";
892 PRINT TAB(INT(Y+15.5));"*"
893 GOTO 895
894 PRINT "....X AXIS IS LIGHT INTENSITY......*..."
895 NEXT X
896 U=0
897 PRINT
898 RETURN
899 REM
900 REM L INPUT SUBROUTINE
902 PRINT "WHAT IS THE NEW DISTANCE FROM SLITS TO"
903 PRINT "SCREEN (L) IN METERS";
904 INPUT L
905 REM 1000 CONVERTS METERS TO MILLIMETERS
906 IF 1000*L>=10*D THEN 912
907 PRINT "THIS DISTANCE IS TOO SMALL FOR GOOD"
908 PRINT "INTERFERENCE PATTERNS.  TRY AGAIN."
910 GOTO 902
912 IF L<=5 THEN 918
913 PRINT "ALTHOUGH ANY DISTANCE LARGER THAN"
914 PRINT 10*D/1000;"METERS IS VALID, ABOVE 5 METERS"
915 PRINT "BECOMES HARD TO SEE.  TRY ANOTHER VALUE."
916 GOTO 902
918 RETURN
919 REM
920 REM D INPUT SUBROUTINE
922 PRINT "WHAT IS THE NEW SLIT SEPARATION (D) IN"
923 PRINT "MILLIMETERS";
924 INPUT D
926 IF D>=.1 THEN 932
928 PRINT "SLITS ARE SO CLOSE THEY APPROXIMATE A"
929 PRINT "SINGLE SLIT.  TRY ANOTHER VALUE."
930 GOTO 922
932 IF D<=.1*1000*L THEN 940
933 PRINT "FOR A VALID INTERFERENCE PATTERN, THE"
934 PRINT "SEPARATION SHOULD BE LESS THAN";.1*1000*L
935 PRINT "MILLIMETERS.  TRY ANOTHER VALUE."
938 GOTO 922
940 RETURN
941 REM
942 REM W INPUT SUBROUTINE
944 PRINT "WHAT IS THE NEW WAVELENGTH (W) IN"
945 PRINT "ANGSTROMS";
946 INPUT W
947 IF W>=3000 THEN 954
948 IF W<1000 THEN 959
```

```
949 PRINT "A WAVELENGTH OF";W;"IS ULTRAVIOLET"
950 PRINT "LIGHT AND NOT VISIBLE."
951 GOTO 956
954 IF W<=8000 THEN 965
955 PRINT "A WAVELENGTH OF";W;"IS INFRARED LIGHT   AND NOT VISIBLE."
956 PRINT "THE INTERFERENCE PATTERN WILL BE VISIBLEUSING DETECTORS ONLY."
957 PRINT "TRY ANOTHER WAVELENGTH."
958 GOTO 944
959 PRINT "A WAVELENGTH OF";W;"IS X-RAYS AND NOT   VISIBLE."
960 GOTO 956
965 RETURN
966 REM
967 PRINT
968 PRINT "*****"
969 PRINT
970 REM MISCELLANEOUS RUNS
972 PRINT "WOULD YOU LIKE A PLOT WITH YOUR OWN"
973 PRINT "VALUES FOR WAVELENGTH (W), SLIT"
974 PRINT "SEPARATION (D), AND DISTANCE FROM SLITS"
975 PRINT "TO SCREEN (L) (1=YES, 0=NO)";
976 INPUT Q9
980 IF Q9<1 THEN 995
982 GOSUB 944
984 GOSUB 922
986 GOSUB 902
988 GOSUB 855
990 PRINT "ANOTHER ONE (1=YES, 0=NO)";
992 INPUT Q8
993 IF Q8>0 THEN 982
994 REM
995 PRINT
996 PRINT"**********"
997 PRINT
998 PRINT "HOPE YOU HAD FUN!"
999 END
READY.
```

Other Huntington Simulations. These include:

TAG—students study the size of a large-mouth bass population in a pond environment through the technique of tagging and recovery.

RATS—simulation of the rat population in a city or apartment house.

HARDY—investigation of the Hardy-Weinberg Principle.

BUFLO—effects of different harvesting policies on the bison.

MASPAR—simulation of the relationship between social status and membership in organizations, with mass political participation.

SAP—statistical calculations useful for examining and analyzing large quantities of survey data.

MALAR—malaria eradication as a typical world health problem.

POP—population growth modeling with three simple models.

POLSYS—the processes in local government.

CHARGE—the Millikan Oil Drop Experiment.

LOCKEY—the lock and key model of enzyme specificity.

STERL—the use of pesticides and the release of sterile males as methods of pest control.

POLICY—special interest groups and government.
MARKET—two companies compete for market shares of a certain product.
USPOP—human population model of the U.S.
SCATER—alpha particle scattering according to three models.
PH—three laboratory investigations dealing with the pH specificity of enzymes.

Chelsea Science Project

Another source of simulations is the Chelsea Science Project. Six simulations in biology, chemistry, and physics are available:*

EVOLUT—a study of natural selection and differential survival among different organisms.
RKINET—experiments in reaction kinetics.
COEXIST—a study of population dynamics.
LINKOVER—simulated genetic mapping experiments.
NEWTON—Newton's Law of Gravitation and Second Law of Motion.
SCATTER—three nuclear scattering experiments.

Developing Simulations—A Major Investment in Time

Once familiar with the effectiveness of computer simulation, most teachers are anxious to custom-build their own. This is an understandable desire, but developing simulation materials is unbelievably time-consuming. The best available materials have been developed with a ratio of *several hundred* development hours to *one hour* of student material. Developing a simulation from scratch is a tremendous undertaking and shouldn't be attempted without careful, often tedious planning.

As a first step, the learning objectives need to be carefully stated and evaluated. Simulation should be just one of a number of possible instructional strategies considered. Constraints such as time, space, money, and the individuals involved need to be identified. Only after this first step should you decide whether or not your particular situation is an appropriate simulation opportunity.

The next task is overwhelming but critical: A model has to be constructed of the situation being simulated. The developer collects and sorts information, constructs a model or outline, and selects which elements in the real situation will be reproduced in the simulated situation. He or she

*Write Edward Arnold (Publishers) Ltd., Woodlands Park Avenue, Woodlands Park, Maidenhead, Berkshire, England.

must then identify the participants or "actors," their objectives, and their resources. A sequence of events is defined as well as the results of interactions among the actors. Rules are established, and the winning criteria set. Only then is the programmer ready to tackle the job.

Once the simulation is coded and documented, it should be tested on as many students as possible, formally evaluated with regard to its effectiveness in meeting the objectives, and modified as indicated by the test results and other evaluation. At this point, the simulation is ready for widespread use and for export to other locations.

References

Abt, Clark C., *Serious Games*. New York: The Viking Press, Inc., 1970.

Ahl, David H., "How to Write a Computer Simulation," *Proceedings of the Fifth Conference on Computers in the Undergraduate Curricula*, Iowa City, Iowa: Lindquist Center for Measurement, University of Iowa, 1974.

Albert, D., and D. L. Bitzer, "Advances in Computer-Based Instruction," *Science*, 167:1582-1590 (March 20, 1970).

Beaird, J. H., "Learner Variables and the Instructional Technologist," *The Contribution of the Behavioral Sciences to Instructional Technology*. Teaching Research, Oregon State System of Higher Education, 1967.

Bewley, W., D. Holznagel, and D. Klassen, "Toward a Cognitive Developmental Rationale for the Instructional Use of Simulations," *Proceedings of the Second World Conference on Computer Education*. IFIPS, 1975.

Bobula, J. A. and G. G. Page, *Manual on Construction of Written Simulations*. Chicago: Center for Educational Development, University of Illinois College of Medicine, 1973.

Boocock, Sarane S., and E. O. Schild, *Simulation Games in Learning*. Beverly Hills, Cal.: Sage Publications, 1968.

Braun, L., "Digital Simulation in Education," *Journal of Educational Technology Systems* (Winter 1972).

_____, "Learning Through Computer Simulation," presented at the Annual Meeting of the American Educational Research Association, Washington, D.C., March 30-April 3, 1975.

Bushnell, D. D., "Computer Simulation," *Saturday Review*, 49:31 (1966).

Dorn, William S., "Simulation Versus Models: Which One and When?" *Journal of Research in Science Teaching*, Vol. 12, No. 4 (1975).

Edwards, Judith B., "Simulation for Instruction: Some Considerations for Users and Designers," *ACM SIGCUE Bulletin,* Vol. 7, No. 2 (April 1973).

Fletcher, J. L., "The Effectiveness of Simulation Games as Learning Environments," *Simulation and Games*, No. 2 (1975).

Gann, Nigel, "A Teacher's Personal View of Simulation," *Programmed Learning and Educational Technology*, 13:3 (July 1976).

Gordon, Alice Kaplan, *Educational Games Extension Service*. Science Research Associates (1967).

Hulsey, John Adler Jr., "New Insights into Simulation as an Effective Method of Teaching Social Studies," *High School Journal* (February 1977).

Livingston, S. A., "Will a Simulation Game Improve Student Learning of Related Factual Material?" *Educational Technology*, 11:19–20 (December 1971).

_____, and C. S. Stoll, *Simulation Games: An Introduction for the Social Studies Teacher*. New York: The Free Press, 1973.

MacLean, Rupert, "Simulation and Games with Particular Reference to the Teaching of Economics," *Programmed Learning and Educational Technology*, 13:3 (July 1976).

McLean, H., and M. Raymond, *Design Your Own Game*. Lebanon, Ohio: The Simulation and Gaming Association, RR No. 2, Greentree Road.

Meadows, D. H., *et al., The Limits to Growth*. New York: Signet Publications, 1972.

Mize, J. H. and J. G. Cox, *Essentials of Simulation*. Englewood Cliffs, N.J.: Prentice-Hall, Inc., 1968.

Naylor, T. H., *et al., Computer Simulation Techniques*, New York: John Wiley & Sons, Inc., 1968.

Pate, G. S. and H. A. Parker, Jr., *Designing Classroom Simulations*. Belmont, Cal.: Fearon, Inc., 1973.

Visich, Marian, Jr., and Ludwig Braun, "Computer Simulation as an Educational Tool," *Proceedings of the Fifth Conference on Computers in the Undergraduate Curricula*. Iowa City, Iowa: Lindquist Center for Measurement, University of Iowa, 1974.

Watson, Paul G., *Using the Computer in Education*, Educational Technology Publications, 1972.

CHAPTER SEVEN

GAMES

The play world is a magic one, a charmed circle with its own boundaries of space and time, its own rules of acceptable behavior, and a consciousness that it exists apart from the real world.

—Johann Huizinga,
Homo Ludens (1955)

Educational games, particularly those played with the computer, make it possible to bring that magic, at least temporarily, into the classroom. With a little further sleight-of-hand, some of these games can make a real contribution to student attitudes and to their understanding of their subjects.

A good deal of conflict surrounds most discussions of classroom games—especially computerized games. Participants in the debate can't agree on whether there is any redeeming educational value to game-playing. Nor can they decide on how to encourage students to realize that value, if it does indeed exist.

Why Games?

We believe that beyond the motivational value of computer games and in spite of their oft-seeming frivolous nature, games provide the opportunity for an added dimension to classroom teaching—one that is relevant and fun. Many of the world's most famous games exercise skills of logic and observation or impart "second-hand" knowledge of the real world. Think of such diverse games as Monopoly, Mastermind, Clue, Tic-Tac-Toe, and Bridge, as a few examples. None of these has any avowed educational purpose, yet all of them exercise the intellect of the players in one way or another.

Games are valuable in the upbringing of small children because they not only require careful reading and logical thinking, but they also, often quite without design, reinforce number concepts and verbal skills. But the relevance of game-playing is not confined to the very young: Even at the secondary level, there is a need for an occasional break from the serious atmosphere of the typical classroom.

The center of the conflict is just how much learning occurs and whether it is enough to make it worth the trouble. We think that there are a number of reasons to play games in the classroom, even if they are not always "serious" games:

1. Students like them and look forward to them.
2. Games can be played by groups of students as teams, with all the socialization to be gained from competitive interaction among peers. Cooperation is necessary for success and discipline is self-imposed by having to play by the rules. The games are student-centered and student-managed, with little interference from the teacher.
3. Games help develop decision-making capabilities and problem-solving skills, as well as encourage imaginative and creative responses.
4. Games introduce new ideas. They are open-ended and can be modified for use for a multitude of purposes.
5. Games can expand the attention span of students as a result of intense involvement in a goal-directed activity.
6. Games can be made relevant to students' lives or backgrounds, oriented to any chosen problem area, or related to a totally imaginative situation, depending on the desires and needs of the teacher and the students.

Let's look at the game known as Pharaoh's Needles or, more commonly, the Tower of Hanoi.

When you begin the computerized game, from two to seven disks are on the leftmost needle, the largest on the bottom and the smallest on the top. Moving one disk at a time, and never placing a larger one on a smaller one, your object is to move the entire stack of disks to the rightmost needle, again with the largest on the bottom and the smallest on the top.

TOWERS OF HANOI PUZZLE

HOW MANY DISKS DO YOU WANT TO MOVE (7 MAX)? *3*

IN THIS PROGRAM, WE WILL REFER TO THE DISKS
WITH A NUMERICAL CODE. 3 WILL REPRESENT THE
SMALLEST DISK, 5 THE NEXT SIZE, 7 THE NEXT,
AND SO ON, UP TO 15. IF YOU DO THE PUZZLE
WITH 2 DISKS, THEIR CODE NAMES WOULD BE 13
AND 15. WITH THREE DISKS, THE CODE NAMES
WOULD BE 11, 13, AND 15, ETC. NEEDLES ARE

NUMBERED FROM LEFT TO RIGHT, 1 TO 3. WE
WILL START WITH THE DISKS ON NEEDLE 1, AND
ATTEMPT TO MOVE THEM TO NEEDLE 3.

GOOD LUCK!

```
        *              *              *
        *              *              *
  ***********          *              *
  ***********          *              *
 *************         *              *
```

WHICH DISK WOULD YOU LIKE TO MOVE? *11*
PLACE DISK ON WHICH NEEDLE? *3*

```
        *              *              *
        *              *              *
        *              *              *
  ***********          *              *
 *************         *         ***********
```

WHICH DISK WOULD YOU LIKE TO MOVE? *13*
PLACE DISK ON WHICH NEEDLE? *2*

```
        *              *              *
        *              *              *
        *              *              *
        *              *              *
 *************   ************    ***********
```

WHICH DISK WOULD YOU LIKE TO MOVE? *11*
PLACE DISK ON WHICH NEEDLE? *2*

```
        *              *              *
        *              *              *
        *              *              *
        *        ***********          *
 *************   ************         *
```

WHICH DISK WOULD YOU LIKE TO MOVE? *15*
PLACE DISK ON WHICH NEEDLE? *3*

```
        *              *              *
        *              *              *
        *              *              *
        *        ***********          *
        *        ************   **************
```

WHICH DISK WOULD YOU LIKE TO MOVE? *11*
PLACE DISK ON WHICH NEEDLE? *1*

```
        *              *              *
        *              *              *
        *              *              *
        *              *              *
  ***********    ************   **************
```

WHICH DISK WOULD YOU LIKE TO MOVE? *13*
PLACE DISK ON WHICH NEEDLE? *3*

```
        *              *              *
        *              *              *
        *              *              *
        *              *         ************
  ***********          *         **************
```

WHICH DISK WOULD YOU LIKE TO MOVE? *11*
PLACE DISK ON WHICH NEEDLE? *3*

```
    *                *                *
    *                *                *
    *                *                *
    *                *         **********
    *                *         ************
    *                *         **************
```

CONGRATULATIONS!! YOU HAVE PERFORMED THE
TASK IN 7 MOVES.

Now this is not an obviously educational game. Yet it is definitely
an intellectual exercise. First, when the instructions are printed out in full
(we left some of them out), the student learns the legend of the monks that
live under the city of Hanoi. Second, he or she learns the code mechanism
and how to manipulate the disks. Third, the student must very logically
plan the moves, since there is only one strategy that accomplishes the task in
the fewest possible moves. We think it is clear that students benefit from
this kind of mental gymnastics; it sharpens their logical thinking and
teaches them patience.

Kinds of Games

There are any number of ways to classify games: by the number of
players, by the medium used, by the knowledge required, by the subject at
stake, and so forth. We choose to introduce you to the "family" groupings
used by David H. Ahl in his book *101 BASIC Computer Games*. Ahl's
categories are (1) guessing games, (2) piles of objects, (3) matrix, (4)
history/government, (5) logic, (6) gambling, (7) card and board, (8) sports,
(9) space, (10) war, (11) word, and (12) date games. The games in this
chapter fit into these categories, although not all categories are represented.

Sources of Games

Ahl's book is one of the best sources of computer games—we
especially like its organization and breadth of coverage. Since publishing
101, Ahl has founded the most popular educational/recreational magazine
in the industry, *Creative Computing*, which is itself a continuing source of
games. Another "super" collection of games, although there is some
overlap, is *What To Do When You Hit Return*, written by People's
Computer Company and published jointly with Hewlett-Packard. PCC and
friends now publish three magazines devoted to home/school computing,
which are described in Chapter 10 and listed in the reference section at the
end of this chapter.

Guessing Games

The first game programmed on our PET was a simpleminded number guessing game. All it did was check for the right number between 1 and 10, and a BREAK was required to stop the program.

> GUESS A NUMBER BETWEEN 1 AND 10
> ?3
> SORRY, YOU'RE WRONG
> GUESS AGAIN.
> ?5
> SORRY, YOU'RE WRONG
> GUESS AGAIN
> ?7
> WHAT A SMART KID! HERE'S ANOTHER ONE
> GUESS A NUMBER BETWEEN 1 AND 10
> ?8
> SORRY, YOU'RE WRONG
> BREAK IN 60

The code was very simple:

```
READY.
 1 REM SIMGUESS
10 X=INT(RND(.5)*10+1)
20 PRINT "GUESS A NUMBER BETWEEN 1 AND 10"
30 INPUT A
40 IF A=X GOTO 60
50 PRINT "SORRY, YOU'RE WRONG"
53 PRINT "GUESS AGAIN"
55 GOTO 30
60 PRINT "WHAT A SMART KID! HERE'S ANOTHER ONE"
65 GOTO 10
70 END
READY.
```

Primitive it was, but we had it running about two minutes after we first plugged in the PET; and it continues to enthrall preschool kids who can't read more complicated messages. Half an hour later, we dashed off a better version that allowed us to set the range of numbers and that told us whether our guess was too high or too low:

> WHAT IS THE TOP NUMBER IN THE
> RANGE YOU WISH TO GUESS?
> ?10

I HAVE A NUMBER BETWEEN 1 AND 10.
CAN YOU GUESS IT? *5*
NO, YOUR GUESS IS TOO LOW. GUESS AGAIN.
?*7*
?NO, YOUR GUESS IS TOO HIGH. GUESS AGAIN.
?*6*
YOU GUESSED IT!

Next—competitive people that we are—we wanted to keep track of the number of tries, so that we could see who guessed most quickly. Here's our final version:

WHAT IS THE TOP NUMBER IN THE
RANGE YOU WISH TO GUESS?
?*10*
OK. I HAVE A NUMBER BETWEEN 1 AND 10
CAN YOU GUESS IT?
?*5*
NO, YOUR GUESS IS TOO LOW. GUESS AGAIN.
?*8*
NO, YOUR GUESS IS TOO HIGH. GUESS AGAIN.
?*7*
YOU GUESSED IT! IT TOOK YOU 3 TRIES
DO YOU WANT TO TRY ANOTHER?

The program looks like this:

```
READY.

10 REM NUMBER GUESSING GAME
20 PRINT "WHAT IS THE TOP NUMBER IN THE"
30 PRINT "RANGE YOU WISH TO GUESS?"
40 INPUT T
50 REM PICK A NUMBER IN THAT RANGE
60 X=INT(RND(TI)*T)+1
70 REM ALLOW GUESSING
80 PRINT "OK. I HAVE A NUMBER BETWEEN 1 AND ";T;".
90 PRINT "CAN YOU GUESS IT?"
100 INPUT G
110 E=E+1
120 IF G=X THEN 150
130 IF G>X THEN PRINT "NO, YOUR GUESS IS TOO HIGH. GUESS AGAIN.":GOTO 100
140 IF G<X THEN PRINT "NO, YOUR GUESS IS TOO LOW. GUESS AGAIN.":GOTO 100
150 PRINT "YOU GUESSED IT! IT TOOK YOU ";E;" TRIES"
155 PRINT "DO YOU WANT TO TRY ANOTHER";
156 E=0
160 INPUT A$
170 IF A$="YES" THEN 20
180 END
READY.
```

Piles of Objects

These games are played with a pile of objects and two players (or with one player and the computer). One well-known variety is 23 Matches, where each player can take 1, 2, or 3 matches when it is his or her turn. You begin with 23 matches, and the goal is to avoid taking the last match:

> WE START WITH 23 MATCHES ON A TABLE.
> YOU MOVE FIRST. YOU MAY TAKE 1, 2, OR 3
> MATCHES, THEN IT'S MY TURN. WHOEVER
> TAKES THE LAST MATCH LOSES.
> HINT: IF YOU MOVE CORRECTLY ON THE
> FIRST MOVE, YOU CAN WIN THE GAME.
>
> THERE ARE NOW 23 MATCHES.
> HOW MANY DO YOU TAKE? *3*
>
> I TOOK 3...THERE ARE NOW 17 MATCHES.
> HOW MANY DO YOU TAKE? *1*
>
> I TOOK 3...THERE ARE NOW 13 MATCHES.
> HOW MANY DO YOU TAKE? *2*
>
> I TOOK 2...THERE ARE NOW 9 MATCHES.
> HOW MANY DO YOU TAKE? *1*
>
> I TOOK 3...THERE ARE NOW 5 MATCHES.
> HOW MANY DO YOU TAKE? *1*
>
> I TOOK 3...THERE IS NOW 1 MATCH.
> HOW MANY DO YOU TAKE? *1*
> I WON!!!BETTER LUCK NEXT TIME!

Here is the listing:

```
READY.

10 REM MATCHES GAME
20 PRINT "WE START WITH 23 MATCHES ON A TABLE."
30 PRINT "YOU MOVE FIRST. YOU MAY TAKE 1,2, OR 3"
40 PRINT "MATCHES, THEN IT'S MY TURN. WHOEVER"
50 PRINT "TAKES THE LAST MATCH LOSES."
55 PRINT "HINT: IF YOU MOVE CORRECTLY ON THE"
60 PRINT "FIRST MOVE, YOU CAN WIN THE GAME."
70 PRINT:M=23
80 REM PLAYER ASKED TO MOVE
89 IF M=1 THEN 95
```

```
90 PRINT:PRINT"THERE ARE NOW ";M;" MATCHES.";
91 GOTO 100
95 PRINT:PRINT "THERE IS NOW ";M;"MATCH."
100 PRINT
105 PRINT "HOW MANY DO YOU TAKE";:INPUT P
110 IF P>M THEN 340
120 IF P<>INT(P) THEN 340
130 IF P<=0 THEN 340
140 IF P>3 THEN 340
150 LET M=M-P
160 IF M=0 THEN 290
170 REM NOW IT'S THE COMPUTER'S TURN
180 IF M=1 THEN 310
190 R=M-4*INT(M/4)
200 IF R<>1 THEN 230
210 C=INT(3*RND(TI))+1
220 GOTO 240
230 C=(R+3)-4*INT((R+3)/4)
240 M=M-C
250 IF M=0 THEN 310
255 IF C=1 THEN 275
260 PRINT:PRINT"I TOOK ";C;"MATCHES."
270 GOTO 89
275 PRINT:PRINT "I TOOK ";C;"MATCH."
276 GOTO 89
280 REM WHO'S THE WINNER???
290 PRINT:PRINT"I WON! BETTER LUCK NEXT TIME!"
300 GOTO 70
310 PRINT:PRINT"SHUCKS, YOU WON! I WANT ANOTHER CHANCE"
320 GOTO 70
330 REM SCOLD PLAYER
340 PRINT"YOU CHEATED! FOLLOW THE RULES!"
350 GOTO 100
READY.
```

There are more difficult games available that follow the same principle.

Matrix Games

Our favorite matrix (or grid) game is Mugwump, where four mugwumps are hiding in a 10 × 10 matrix. (Yes, of course, we know what a mugwump is . . . don't you?) You begin by guessing a location, then the computer tells you how far away each mugwump is in units on a straight line between the two points. You have ten turns to find all four mugwumps.

THE OBJECT OF THIS GAME IS TO FIND
FOUR MUGWUMPS HIDDEN ON A 10 BY 10
GRID. HOMEBASE IS POSITION 0,0.
ANY GUESS YOU MAKE MUST BE TWO
NUMBERS, EACH BETWEEN 0 AND 9.
THE FIRST NUMBER IS THE DISTANCE
TO THE RIGHT OF HOMEBASE AND THE
SECOND NUMBER IS THE DISTANCE ABOVE
HOMEBASE.

YOU GET 10 TRIES. AFTER EACH TRY,
I WILL TELL YOU HOW FAR YOU ARE
FROM EACH MUGWUMP.

TURN NO. 1. WHAT IS YOUR GUESS? *5,5*
YOU ARE 6.4 UNITS FROM MUGWUMP 1
YOU ARE 1.4 UNITS FROM MUGWUMP 2
YOU ARE 2.2 UNITS FROM MUGWUMP 3
YOU ARE 1.4 UNITS FROM MUGWUMP 4

TURN NO. 2. WHAT IS YOUR GUESS? *4,4*
YOU ARE 5 UNITS FROM MUGWUMP 1
YOU ARE 2 UNITS FROM MUGWUMP 2
YOU ARE 1 UNIT FROM MUGWUMP 3
YOU ARE 2.8 UNITS FROM MUGWUMP 4

TURN NO. 3. WHAT IS YOUR GUESS? *6,6*
YOU ARE 7.8 UNITS FROM MUGWUMP 1
YOU ARE 2 UNITS FROM MUGWUMP 2
YOU ARE 3.6 UNITS FROM MUGWUMP 3
YOU HAVE FOUND MUGWUMP 4

.
.
.

and so forth.

This game is good reinforcement for two key concepts in geometry:
first the Pythagorean Theorem and, second, the position of points on a
coordinate plane. *Hint:* The game is much less frustrating if you use graph
paper to keep track of your guesses and of the location of each mugwump
that you find.
    The listing follows:

```
READY.
  10 REM HUNT THE MUGWUMP GAME
  20 REM FIRST, THE INSTRUCTIONS
  30 PRINT "THE OBJECT OF THIS GAME IS TO FIND "
  31 PRINT"FOUR MUGWUMPS HIDDEN ON A 10 BY 10 "
  32 PRINT"GRID. HOMEBASE IS POSITION 0,0. "
  33 PRINT"ANY GUESS YOU MAKE MUST BE TWO "
  34 PRINT"NUMBERS, EACH BETWEEN 0 AND 9. "
  35 PRINT"THE FIRST NUMBER IS THE DISTANCE "
  36 PRINT"TO THE RIGHT OF HOMEBASE AND THE "
  37 PRINT"SECOND NUMBER IS THE DISTANCE ABOVE "
  38 PRINT"HOMEBASE."
  39 PRINT
  50 PRINT"YOU GET  10 TRIES. AFTER EACH TRY, "
```

```
51 PRINT"I WILL TELL YOU HOW FAR YOU ARE "
52 PRINT"FROM EACH MUGWUMP."
53 PRINT
100 GOSUB 1000
110 T=0
120 T=T+1
130 PRINT:PRINT
140 PRINT"TURN NO. ";T;" WHAT IS YOUR GUESS";
150 INPUT M,N
160 FOR I=1 TO 4
170 IF P(I,1)=-1 THEN 250
180 IF P(I,1)<>M THEN 230
190 IF P(I,2)<>N THEN 230
200 P(I,1)=-1
210 PRINT"YOU HAVE FOUND MUGWUMP";I
220 GOTO 250
230 D=SQR((P(I,1)-M)↑2+(P(I,2)-N)↑2)
240 PRINT"YOU ARE ";INT(D*100)/100;"UNITS FROM MUGWUMP"I
250 NEXT I
260 FOR J=1 TO 4
270 IF P(J,1)<>-1 THEN 310
280 NEXT J
290 PRINT:PRINT"YOU GOT THEM ALL IN";T;"TURNS!"
300 GOTO 380
310 IF T<10 THEN 120
320 PRINT:PRINT"SORRY, YOU'VE RUN OUT OF TURNS."
330 PRINT"HERE IS WHERE THEY'RE HIDING."
340 FOR I=1 TO 4
350 IF P(I,1)=-1 THEN 370
360 PRINT"MUGWUMP";I;"IS AT (";P(I,1);",";P(I,2);")"
370 NEXT I
380 PRINT:PRINT"THAT WAS FUN! LET'S PLAY AGAIN..."
390 PRINT"FOUR MORE MUGWUMPS ARE HIDING."
400 GOTO 100
1000 FOR I=1 TO 4
1010 FOR J=1 TO 2
1020 P(I,J)=INT(10*RND(TI))
1030 NEXT J
1034 IF I=1 GOTO 1040
1035 FOR K=1 TO I-1
1036 IF P(K,1)=P(I,1) AND P(K,2)=P(I,2)GOTO 1010
1037 NEXT K
1040 NEXT I
1050 RETURN
1099 END
READY.
```

Note that there is no check that the entered numbers are between 0 and 9. One of our friends noticed this oversight while playing the game and found a sneaky way to guess all four mugwumps in six tries.

Logic Games

In one sense, all games can be defined as games of logic, except gambling games which we all know as games of chance. Logic games are without a doubt our favorites—especially the two classics that we include here. At least a dozen other good ones are available in the two books cited as references earlier in the chapter.

BAGLES is a numerical version of the popular game Mastermind. The computer selects a three-digit number, and your goal is to guess that number in as few turns as possible. You are given clues after each turn that tell you how many digits are correct and how many are in the right position. You should be able to deduce the correct number in only six or seven turns once you discover the strategy.

> GAME OF BAGLES—WANT RULES?
> (YES OR NO)? *YES*
>
> I AM THINKING OF A
> THREE DIGIT NUMBER. TRY TO GUESS
> MY NUMBER AND I WILL GIVE YOU
> CLUES ABOUT YOUR GUESS AS FOLLOWS:
> PICO MEANS ONE DIGIT CORRECT
>   BUT IN THE WRONG POSITION
> FERMI MEANS ONE DIGIT CORRECT
>   AND IN THE RIGHT POSITION
> BAGLES MEANS NO DIGITS CORRECT
>
> GUESS A THREE DIGIT NUMBER WITH
> NO TWO DIGITS THE SAME. ANY DIGIT MAY
> BE A 0 (ZERO).
>
> OK. I HAVE A NUMBER IN MIND.
>
> GUESS NO. 1:? 123
>   BAGLES
> GUESS NO. 2:? 456
>   FERMI
> GUESS NO. 3:? 478
>   FERMI PICO
> GUESS NO. 4:? 479
>   FERMI PICO PICO
> GUESS NO. 5:? 497
>   YOU GUESSED IT! WANT TO PLAY AGAIN?
> (YES OR NO)? NO
> OK, HOPE YOU HAD FUN PLAYING
> WITH ME. SEE YOU LATER.

The algorithm for this game was a little tricky to develop. Here is the listing:

```
5 REM BAGLES NUMBER GUESSING GAME
30 DIM D(3),G(3)
40 PRINT "GAME OF BAGLES. WANT RULES?"
50 INPUT "(YES OR NO)";A$
60 IF A$="NO" THEN 150
70 PRINT:PRINT"I AM THINKING OF A"
```

```
80 PRINT"THREE DIGIT NUMBER. TRY TO GUESS"
90 PRINT"MY NUMBER AND I WILL GIVE YOU "
100 PRINT"CLUES ABOUT YOUR GUESS AS FOLLOWS"
105 PRINT"  PICO MEANS ONE DIGIT CORRECT "
110 PRINT"         BUT IN THE WRONG POSITION"
115 PRINT"  FERMI MEANS ONE DIGIT CORRECT "
120 PRINT"          AND IN THE RIGHT POSITION"
125 PRINT"  BAGLES MEANS NO DIGITS CORRECT ": PRINT
126 PRINT"GUESS A THREE DIGIT NUMBER, WITH"
127 PRINT"NO TWO DIGITS THE SAME.   ANY DIGIT MAY"
128 PRINT "BE A 0 (ZERO)."
130 NG=INT(RND(TI)*1000)
140 D(1)=INT(NG/100)
150 D(2)=INT(NG/10)-D(1)*10
160 D(3)=NG-D(1)*100-D(2)*10
170 IF D(1)=D(2) OR D(2)=D(3) OR D(1)=D(3) THEN 130
180 PRINT:PRINT"OK, I HAVE A NUMBER IN MIND.":PRINT
210 FOR I=1 TO 20
215 F=0:P=0
217 PRINT
220 PRINT"GUESS NO.";I;":";
230 INPUT GS
235 IF GS<>INT(GS) THEN PRINT "YOUR GUESS MUST BE AN INTEGER": GOTO 217
240 IF GS<0  OR GS>999 THEN PRINT "ONLY POSITIVE THREE DIGIT NUMBERS":GOTO 217
250 G(1)=INT(GS/100)
260 G(2)=INT(GS/10)-G(1)*10
270 G(3)=GS-G(1)*100-G(2)*10
275 IF G(1)<>G(2) AND G(1)<>G(3) AND G(2)<>G(3) THEN 280
276 PRINT "YOUR GUESS MUST HAVE NO TWO DIGITS THE  SAME": GOTO 217
280 FOR J=1 TO 3
290 IF G(J)=D(J) THEN F=F+1
300 NEXT J
310 FOR J=1 TO 3
315 FOR K=1 TO3
320 IF J=K THEN 340
330 IF G(J)=D(K) THEN P=P+1
340 NEXT K
350 NEXT J
355 PRINT "              ";
360 IF P+F=0 THEN 430
365 IF F=0 THEN 395
370 FOR J=1 TO F
375 IF F=3 THEN 500
380 PRINT"FERMI ";
390 NEXT J
395 IF P=0 THEN PRINT:GOTO 440
400 FOR J=1 TO P
410 PRINT"PICO ";
420 NEXT J
425 PRINT:GOTO 440
430 PRINT"BAGLES"
440 NEXT I
450 PRINT"WELL, THAT'S YOUR 20 GUESSES.   MY NUMBER WAS:";
460 PRINT STR$(D(1)); STR$(D(2)); STR$(D(3))
470 GOTO 510
500 PRINT"YOU GUESSED IT!!"
510 PRINT"DO YOU WANT TO PLAY AGAIN (YES OR NO)"
515 INPUT A$
520 IF A$="YES" THEN 130
530 PRINT"OK,HOPE YOU HAD FUN PLAYING"
540 PRINT"WITH ME.  SEE YOU LATER."
599 END
```

   The other logic game is called REVERSE. The computer prints out a scrambled list of the integers from 1 to 9. Your goal is to rearrange them into their proper order in as few moves as possible. This rearrangement is accomplished by reversing any number of digits from the left with each move, until the numbers are in sequence.

REVERSE—A GAME OF SKILL

DO YOU WANT THE RULES (YES OR NO)? *YES*

THIS IS THE GAME OF 'REVERSE'. TO WIN,
ALL YOU HAVE TO DO IS ARRANGE A LIST
OF NUMBERS (1 THRU 9) IN NUMERICAL
ORDER FROM LEFT TO RIGHT. TO MOVE, YOU
TELL ME HOW MANY NUMBERS (COUNTING FROM
THE LEFT) TO REVERSE. FOR EXAMPLE, IF
THE CURRENT LIST IS:
2 3 4 5 1 6 7 8 9
AND YOU REVERSE 4, THE RESULT WILL BE:
5 4 3 2 1 6 7 8 9
NOW IF YOU REVERSE 5, YOU WIN!
1 2 3 4 5 6 7 8 9
NO DOUBT YOU WILL LIKE THIS GAME OF
SKILL, BUT IF YOU WANT TO QUIT, REVERSE
0 (ZERO)

HERE WE GO...THE LIST IS

4 1 3 2 7 8 5 9 6

HOW MANY SHALL I REVERSE? *5*

7 2 3 1 4 8 5 9 6

HOW MANY SHALL I REVERSE? (and so on)

.

.

.

HOW MANY SHALL I REVERSE? *6*

1 2 3 4 5 6 7 8 9

YOU WON IN 12 MOVES!!!
TRY AGAIN (YES OR NO)? *NO*

There is a strategy that makes this game very easy, and your performance will be disappointing until you discover it. (Our first game took
44 moves!)

```
100 PRINT
110 PRINT "REVERSE -- A GAME OF SKILL"
120 PRINT
130 DIM A(20)
140 REM *** N=NUMBER OF NUMBERS
```

```
150 N=9
160 INPUT "DO YOU WANT THE RULES (YES OR NO)";A$
180 IF A$="NO" THEN 210
190 GOSUB 710
200 REM *** MAKE A RANDOM LIST A(1) TO A(N)
210 A(1)=INT(N*RND(TI))+1
220 FOR K=2 TO N
230 A(K)=INT(N*RND(TI))+1
240 FOR J=1 TO K-1
250 IF A(K)=A(J) THEN 230
260 NEXT J
270 NEXT K
280 REM *** PRINT ORIGINAL LIST AND START GAME
290 PRINT
300 PRINT "HERE WE GO ... THE LIST IS:"
310 T=0
320 GOSUB 610
330 INPUT "HOW MANY SHALL I REVERSE";R
340 IF R<>INT(R) THEN 330
350 IF R<=0 THEN 560
360 IF R<=N THEN 390
370 PRINT "OOPS!  TOO MANY - ";N;"IS THE MOST I CAN  REVERSE"
380 GOTO 330
390 T=T+1
400 REM *** REVERSE R NUMBERS AND PRINT NEW LIST
410 FOR K=1 TO INT(R/2)
420 Z=A(K)
430 A(K)=A(R-K+1)
440 A(R-K+1)=Z
450 NEXT K
460 GOSUB 610
470 REM *** CHECK FOR A WIN
480 FOR K=1 TO N
490 IF A(K)<>K THEN 330
500 NEXT K
510 PRINT "YOU WON IN";T;"MOVES!!!"
520 PRINT
530 INPUT"TRY AGAIN (YES OR NO)";A$
550 IF A$="YES" THEN 210
560 PRINT
570 PRINT "OK.  HOPE YOU HAD FUN!!"
580 GOTO 999
600 REM *** SUBROUTINE TO PRINT LIST
610 PRINT
620 FOR K=1 TO N
630 PRINT A(K);
640 NEXT K
650 PRINT
660 PRINT
670 RETURN
700 REM *** SUBROUTINE TO PRINT THE RULES
710 PRINT
715 PRINT "THIS IS THE GAME OF 'REVERSE'.  TO WIN,"
720 PRINT "ALL YOU HAVE TO DO IS ARRANGE A LIST"
730 PRINT "OF NUMBERS (1 THRU";N;") IN NUMERICAL"
740 PRINT "ORDER FROM LEFT TO RIGHT.  TO MOVE,YOU"
750 PRINT "TELL ME HOW MANY NUMBERS (COUNTING FROM"
760 PRINT "THE LEFT) TO REVERSE.  FOR EXAMPLE, IF"
770 PRINT "THE CURRENT LIST IS:"
790 PRINT "2 3 4 5 1 6 7 8 9"
800 PRINT
810 PRINT "AND YOU REVERSE 4, THE RESULT WILL BE:"
830 PRINT "5 4 3 2 1 6 7 8 9"
840 PRINT
850 PRINT "NOW, IF YOU REVERSE 5, YOU WIN!"
870 PRINT "1 2 3 4 5 6 7 8 9"
880 PRINT
890 PRINT "NO DOUBT YOU WILL LIKE THIS GAME OF"
900 PRINT "SKILL, BUT IF YOU WANT TO QUIT, REVERSE"
910 PRINT "0 (ZERO)."
920 PRINT
930 RETURN
999 END
READY.
```

Both REVERSE and BAGLES are games of the mind-sharpening variety; while they don't teach a particular topic, they require careful planning and logical thought. They are also played exclusively in competition with oneself, so winning really is measured by improvement—by playing the game in fewer moves than previously.

Gambling Games

Everyone likes to try to outwit Lady Luck. Games of chance are good candidates for computerization, and in fact computer versions of the best-known gambling games are available for many microcomputers. These games are both realistic and fun: craps, blackjack, bingo, roulette, poker, and slot machines have all been successfully implemented on computers.

In the simplified version of craps presented here, the special bets have been eliminated from the game (field bets, hard way bets, big 6 and 8, any craps, and so on). The play of the game is very simple: You begin by "rolling the dice." On the first roll, a 7 or 11 wins for you, and a 2, 3, or 12 loses. Any other number becomes the "point," and you continue to roll until you roll the point again (in which case you win) or until you roll a 7 (in which case you lose and it is the computer's turn to roll the dice).

ARE YOU READY (YES OR NO)? *YES*
SPLENDID!
YOU HAVE 90 DOLLARS TO PLAY WITH.

YOU ROLL FIRST.

HOW MUCH DO YOU BET? *10*

YOU ROLL 5 AND 3 ... SO YOUR POINT IS 8
YOU ROLL 5 AND 6 ... ROLL AGAIN
YOU ROLL 2 AND 2 ... ROLL AGAIN
YOU ROLL 6 AND 2 AND MAKE YOUR POINT

YOU NOW HAVE $100.
HOW MUCH DO YOU BET? *30*

YOU ROLL 6 AND 6 AND CRAP OUT

YOU NOW HAVE $70.
HOW MUCH DO YOU BET? *0*

THANKS FOR THE GAME ... AND
CONGRATULATIONS FOR BEING ABLE TO QUIT
WHILE YOU WERE AHEAD.

The listing looks like this:

```
10 PRINT
100 PRINT "WELCOME TO THE GAME OF CRAPS, WITH ME"
110 PRINT "AS YOUR OPPONENT.  THE RULES ARE SIMPLE"
120 PRINT
130 PRINT "  A 7 OR 11 ON THE FIRST ROLL WINS"
140 PRINT "  A 2, 3, OR 12 ON THE FIRST ROLL LOSES"
150 PRINT
160 PRINT "ANY OTHER NUMBER ROLLED BECOMES YOUR"
170 PRINT "'POINT', AND YOU CONTINUE TO ROLL.  IF"
180 PRINT "YOU ROLL YOUR POINT BEFORE ROLLING A 7,"
184 PRINT "YOU WIN.  BUT IF YOU ROLL A 7 BEFORE"
185 PRINT "YOUR POINT, YOU LOSE, AND THE DICE"
186 PRINT "CHANGE HANDS.  JUST BET $0 TO QUIT."
190 PRINT
200 PRINT
215 INPUT "ARE YOU READY (YES OR NO)";B$
216 IF B$<>"YES" THEN 10
220 PRINT "SPLENDID!     ";
224 Z=5*INT(10+11*RND(TI))
225 PRINT "YOU HAVE";Z;"DOLLARS TO PLAY WITH."
230 PRINT
240 PRINT
250 IF RND(TI)<.5 THEN 310
260 W=-1
270 PRINT "I'LL ROLL FIRST"
300 GOTO 330
310 W=1
320 PRINT "YOU ROLL FIRST"
330 PRINT
340 PRINT
350 Q=0
360 INPUT "HOW MUCH DO YOU BET";B
380 PRINT
390 IF B=INT(B) THEN 430
400 PRINT
410 PRINT "NO COINS, PLEASE.  BILLS ONLY."
420 GOTO 360
430 IF B<=0 THEN 1090
440 IF B<=Z THEN 470
450 PRINT "NO COUNTERFEIT MONEY ALLOWED.  YOU CAN"
455 PRINT "ONLY BET WITH THE MONEY I GAVE YOU."
460 GOTO 360
470 D1=INT(6*RND(TI)+1)
480 D2=INT(6*RND(TI)+1)
490 Q=Q+1
500 S=D1+D2
510 IF W>0 THEN 540
520 PRINT "  I ROLL";D1;"AND";D2;
530 GOTO 550
540 PRINT "  YOU ROLL";D1;"AND";D2;
550 IF Q<>1 THEN 860
560 IF S=2 OR S=3 OR S=12 THEN 640
570 IF S=7 OR S=11 THEN 710
580 IF W>0 THEN 610
590 PRINT "SO MY POINT IS";S
600 GOTO 620
610 PRINT "SO YOUR POINT IS";S
620 P=S
630 GOTO 470
640 PRINT "AND CRAP OUT"
650 C=1
660 IF W>0 THEN 690
670 Z=Z+B
680 GOTO 770
690 Z=Z-B
700 GOTO 770
710 PRINT "AND PASS"
720 C=1
```

```
730 IF W>0 THEN 760
740 Z=Z-B
750 GOTO 770
760 Z=Z+B
770 PRINT
780 IF Z<1 THEN 1060
790 PRINT "YOU NOW HAVE";Z;"DOLLARS"
800 IF C>0 THEN 830
810 PRINT "CHANGE DICE NOW"
820 PRINT
830 W=W*C
840 Q=0
850 GOTO 360
860 IF S<>7 THEN 940
870 PRINT "AND LOSE"
880 C=-1
890 IF W>0 THEN 920
900 Z=Z+B
910 GOTO 770
920 Z=Z-B
930 GOTO 770
940 IF S=P THEN 970
950 PRINT "    ROLL AGAIN"
960 GOTO 470
970 IF W>0 THEN 1020
980 PRINT "AND MAKE MY POINT"
990 C=1
1000 Z=Z-B
1010 GOTO 770
1020 PRINT "AND MAKE YOUR POINT"
1030 C=1
1040 Z=Z+B
1050 GOTO 770
1060 PRINT
1070 PRINT "YOU HAVE RUN OUT OF MONEY....SORRY"
1080 PRINT "ABOUT THAT.  BUT SINCE I PRINT MY OWN,"
1085 PRINT "I'LL GIVE YOU SOME MORE."
1086 GOTO 224
1090 PRINT "THANKS FOR THE GAME....AND"
1100 PRINT "CONGRATULATIONS FOR BEING ABLE TO QUIT"
1110 PRINT "WHILE YOU WERE AHEAD."
1130 END
READY.
```

We can't offhand think of any redeeming social or educational value of the game of craps—but it sure is fun, whether or not the money is real, and your students will love it!

Word Games

Another category of games, word games, can reinforce spelling skills and new vocabulary words. We programmed one very well-known game, only to be criticized by some people for encouraging children in the direction of violence. What can we say? The outcome of the game is no more disastrous than that of a civil war simulation or of a game based on the life and trials of a serf in the Middle Ages.

Our version of HANGMAN allows for both a child's game and an adult game (labeled "Easy" and "Harder" in the output). In the adult game, the computer prints out spaces that correspond to the number of letters in the word it has chosen from an array of words; the player then guesses one letter at a time. If the letter guessed is in the word, it appears in the correct position in the line of spaces. If the letter guessed is wrong, a stick figure's head appears under the scaffold drawn on the screen. The next wrong guess produces the neck, then an arm, and so forth. When the figure is complete (in nine wrong guesses), the player loses and is told the word.

In the child's version, if one letter occurs more than once in the word, when the child guesses that letter it appears in all places. Also, the words can be chosen from a common set of objects, for example, from the furniture in the family room, and a hint is given.

HANGMAN "SPOT" DRAWINGS...

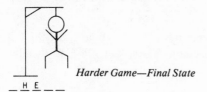

Harder Game—Final State

SORRY.
YOU'RE A GONER!!! THE WORD
WAS 'CHEEK.'

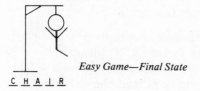

Easy Game—Final State

TODAY'S WORDS ARE FROM
THE FAMILY ROOM.

YOU GUESSED IT!!!

This program is very PET-specific in its use of graphics characters, screen and cursor control characters, the SPC command, and the GET command. Normally, characters are black on a white background, but the terms "inverse" or "inverse video" refer to white characters on a black background. In this way, the special screen control characters are displayed in a listing, as follows:

Clear the screen—is displayed as an inverse heart;
Home the cursor—is displayed as an inverse S;
Move the cursor down 1 line—is displayed as an inverse Q;
Move the cursor up 1 line—is displayed as an inverse solid circle;
Move the cursor forward 1 space, without changing the character displayed in that space (if any)—is displayed as an inverse right-hand bracket;
Move the cursor back 1 space, without changing the character displayed in that space (if any)—is displayed as an inverse vertical line.

You will see these characters printed on the listing that follows. The SPC command is used as:

PRINT SPC (X)

and causes X spaces to be printed. The GET command differs from the INPUT command as follows:

1. It accepts only one character of input, without the need for a carriage return.

2. It does not wait for input but immediately returns with a character, if any has been input.

3. If there has been no character input at the keyboard, a GET C$ statement results in C$ being a null string. Thus, the GET is usually programmed in a loop to wait for input:

10 GET C$
20 IF C$ = "" GOTO 10

4. While the loop executes, no cursor is visible.

5. When a character is input, it is not automatically printed on the screen; and thus the cursor position does not advance. (Remember that the cursor is invisible at this point, but it still has a position where it would appear if it were visible.) If the character is to be printed, the program must do it directly:

10 GET C$
20 IF C$ = "" GOTO 10
30 PRINT C$

With this explanation, the listing should be readable:

```
READY.

10 REM "HANGMAN GAME"
20 DIM A$(150),L$(20),LU(20),WU(150)
30 READ NA,NK
40 GOSUB 850
50 PRINT"⊐INPUT C FOR CHILD'S GAME"
60 PRINT"   OR A FOR ADULT'S GAME"
70 GET M$
71 IF M$="" GOTO 70
80 IF M$<>"A" AND M$<>"C" GOTO 50
90 IF M$="A" GOTO 150
100 NA=NK
110 READ S$
120 GOSUB 850
150 NU=0
```

```
160 NU=NU+1
165 PRINT"◻"
166 IF M$="C" THEN PRINT SPC(15);"TODAY'S WORDS ARE FROM:◼";SPC(95);S$
170 IF NU<=NA GOTO 210
180 PRINT"◼◼◼◼◼YOU HAVE EXHAUSTED ALL MY WORDS"
190 PRINT"I'M TIRED AND I QUIT!"
200 GOTO 9990
210 K=INT(RND(TI)*NA)+1
220 IF WU(K)<>0 GOTO 210
230 WU(K)=1
240 W$=A$(K)
250 NC=LEN(W$)
255 BL=0
260 FOR J=1 TO NC
270 L$(J)=" "
280 LU(J)=0
285 IF MID$(W$,J,1)=" " THEN BL=BL+1
290 NEXT J
300 NG=0
310 NB=0
320 PRINT"◼◼─────┐ "
330 PRINT"        | "
340 PRINT"        | "
350 IF NB=0 GOTO 510
360 PRINT"       ╭─╮ "
370 PRINT"       ╰─╯ "
380 IF NB=1 GOTO 510
390 PRINT"        | "
400 IF NB=2 GOTO 510
410 PRINT"      ─┼";
420 IF NB=3 GOTO 510
430 PRINT"─"
440 IF NB=4 GOTO 510
450 PRINT"        | "
460 PRINT"       ╭─ "
470 IF NB=5 GOTO 510
480 PRINT"        | "
490 IF NB=6 GOTO 510
495 PRINT"        | "
496 IF NB=7 GOTO 510
500 PRINT"◼◼◼◼◼◼◼| "
505 IF NB=8 GOTO 510
506 PRINT"◼◼◼◼◼◼| "
510 PRINT
515 PRINT"◼",SPC(250),SPC(250),SPC(250)
520 PRINT
530 FOR J=1 TO NC
540 PRINT L$(J);" ";
550 NEXT J
560 PRINT
570 FOR J=1 TO NC
580 PRINT "─ ";
585 IF MID$(W$,J,1)=" " THEN PRINT "◼◼◼ ";
590 NEXT J
600 PRINT
605 PRINT"◼",SPC(250),SPC(140),"          ◼◼◼◼◼◼◼◼◼◼◼";
610 IF NB=9 GOTO 650
620 IF NG<>NC-BL GOTO 690
630 PRINT "YOU GOT 'EM ALL!";SPC(24);"FANTASTIC!"
635 FOR J=1 TO 4000: NEXT J
640 GOTO 160
650 PRINT"YOU'RE A GONER!"
660 PRINT SPC(20);"BETTER LUCK NEXT"
670 PRINT SPC(20);"TIME.  THE WORD WAS:";SPC(20);W$
675 FOR J=1 TO 4000: NEXT J
680 GOTO 160
690 PRINT "GUESS A LETTER"
700 GETG$
701 IF G$=""GOTO700
705 PRINT"◼",SPC(250),SPC(100),"          ◼◼◼◼◼◼◼◼◼◼◼",
```

```
706 IF G$=" " GOTO 800
710 SG=NG
720 FOR J=1 TO NC
730 IF LU(J) OR G$<>MID$(W$,J,1) GOTO 780
740 L$(J)=MID$(W$,J,1)
750 LU(J)=1
760 NG=NG+1
770 IF M$="A" GOTO 830
780 NEXT J
790 IF SG<>NG GOTO 830
800 NB=NB+1
810 PRINT "SORRY."
820 GOTO 320
830 PRINT"GOOD GUESS!"
840 GOTO 320
850 FOR J=1 TO NA
660 READ A$(J)
870 NEXT J
880 RETURN
9990 END
10000 DATA 9,5
10001 DATA STARTS,HOSE,NEVERLAND,SHORT
10002 DATA SMARTER,SCOUT,CHILDREN,CHEEK
10003 DATA GOOD
10004 DATA"THE FAMILY ROOM"
10005 DATA CHAIR,COUCH,TV,"COFFEE TABLE"
10006 DATA TOYS
READY.
```

The Game of Life

In the basic game of Life, the invention of a man named John Conway, the user specifies an initial colony of cells on a grid; the computer then generates successive generations of the colony according to the following rules:

    1. An existing cell will die in the next generation if:
        a. it has fewer than two neighboring cells (isolation), or
        b. it has more than three neighboring cells (overpopulation).
    2. An empty space in the grid will produce a birth cell in the next generation if it has exactly three neighboring cells.

Note that each space in the grid has eight neighboring spaces (top, bottom, both sides, and four corners) and that all births and deaths occur simultaneously: A birth cell isn't counted as a neighbor until the next generation, and a dying cell *is* counted until the next generation. For example:

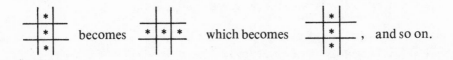

The goal is simple: See what marvelous creations result from your initial colony.

The program listed here, again, is very PET-specific. The user clears the screen, enters an initial colony of cells anywhere except on the top line (using the solid circle graphic character), "HOMEs" the cursor, and enters RUN. The program then asks for the number of desired generations and begins processing. Each dying cell is marked with an X and each birth cell with a B before displaying the next generation. Each generation takes about a minute due to the slow nature of interpreters like BASIC.

Other PET-specific features of this program are:

1. Use of the ASC(C$) function, which returns the internal code for C$. Line 43 is looking for a carriage return, which has a code of 13.

2. Use of the VAL(C$) function, which returns the numeric value of C$. Line 44 calculates the number of generations as the number is entered.

3. Use of the STR$(X) function, which returns a character string for the numeric value X.

4. Use of the PEEK(X) function, which returns the contents of the byte at location X. Note that the screen is addressable at the 1,000 locations starting at 32768. Thus, the first execution of line 100 is to inspect the contents of the top left-hand location of the screen. Note the following screen codes:

Code	Character
81	• (solid circle, indicating a cell)
32	blank (indicating no cell)
86	X (indicating a dying cell)
2	B (indicating a cell being born)

5. Use of the POKE X,Y function, which places the value Y in the byte at address X.

The program decides how many neighbors each grid position has in the following manner: Each grid position in turn is considered to be at position 5 of this layout:

```
1  4  7
2  5  8
3  6  9
```

N1 is calculated to be the number of neighbors in locations 1, 2, and 3; N2 is the number of neighbors in 4, 5, and 6; and N3, in 7, 8, and 9. NN is the total number of neighbors and the sum of N1, N2, and N3. (Since NN includes location 5, which is the location under consideration, line 280 checks for cell death using "less-than-three" and "greater-than-four" comparisons for isolation and overpopulation.) Using this technique reduces neighbor calculation, because when the next grid position is considered (location 8 on the above layout), the old N2 becomes the new N1 and the old N3 becomes the new N2. It is therefore necessary to calculate only a new N3. The listing follows:

```
READY.
   10 REM GAME OF LIFE
   20 B=32768
   30 PRINT"█HOW MANY GENERATIONS? ";
   40 NG=0
   41 GET N$
   42 IF N$="" GOTO 41
   43 IF ASC(N$)=13 GOTO 50
   44 NG=NG*10+VAL(N$)
   45 PRINT N$;
   46 GOTO 41
   50 FOR J=1 TO NG
   60 PRINT"█GENERATION #";STR$(J);" OF";STR$(NG);"      "
   70 FOR I=B+40 TO B+400 STEP 40
   80 N2=0
   90 N3=0
  100 IF PEEK(I-40)>80 THEN N3=N3+1
  110 IF PEEK(I)>80 THEN N3=N3+1
  120 IF PEEK(I+40)>80 THEN N3=N3+1
  130 FOR K=I TO I+9
  140 N1=N2
  150 N2=N3
  160 N3=0
  170 IF K=I+39 GOTO 210
  180 IF PEEK(K-39)>80 THEN N3=N3+1
  190 IF PEEK(K+1)>80 THEN N3=N3+1
  200 IF PEEK(K+41)>80 THEN N3=N3+1
  210 NN=N1+N2+N3
  270 IF PEEK(K)=32 GOTO 300
  280 IF NN<3 OR NN>4 THEN POKE K,86
  290 GOTO 305
  300 IF NN=3 THEN POKE K,2
  305 NEXT K
  310 NEXT I
  320 FOR I=B+40 TO B+409
  330 IF PEEK(I)=2 THEN POKE I,81
  340 IF PEEK(I)=86 THEN POKE I,32
  350 NEXT I
  360 NEXT J
  370 GOTO 30
  380 END
READY.
```

More Games

Other games to be found (with listings) in Ahl's book are: Checkers, baseball, football, basketball, hockey, Bingo, Blackjack, World War II bombing mission, a calendar generator for any year since 1582, Civil War battle strategies, Gomoko, a reign as king of the ancient city-state of Sumeria, Monopoly, a moon landing, Russian Roulette, and Spacewar—to name just a few of the 108 listings. Other games can be found in the references for this chapter. See Chapter 10 for listings and descriptions of periodicals and subscription information.

References

Abt, Clark C., *Serious Games*. New York: The Viking Press, Inc., 1970.

Ahl, David H., *101 BASIC Computer Games*. Maynard, Mass.: Digital Equipment Corporation, 1973.

Gardner, Martin, *Scientific American Book of Mathematical Puzzles and Diversions*. New York: Simon and Schuster, Inc., 1964.

Sage, Edwin, *Fun and Games with the Computer*. Newburyport, Mass.: Entelek, 1974.

Seymour, Dale and Richard Gidley, *Eureka*. Palo Alto, Cal.: Creative Publications, 1967.

Spencer, Donald D., *Game Playing with BASIC*. Rochelle Park, N.J.: Hayden Book Co., Inc., 1977.

Spencer, Donald D., *Game Playing with Computers* (2nd ed.). Rochelle Park, N.J.: Hayden Book Co., Inc., 1975.

What to Do When You Hit Return or PCC's First Book of Computer Games. Hewlett-Packard and People's Computer Company, 1975.

Zuckerman, D. and R. Horn, *The Guide to Simulations/Games for Education and Training*. Lexington, Mass.: Lexington Resources, Inc., 1973.

CHAPTER EIGHT

COMPUTER-ASSISTED INSTRUCTION (CAI)

When computers were first considered for use in schools, they were seen as a means of finally offering every student the one-to-one discovery dialogue found to be effective since ancient times. The early development of computer-assisted instruction (CAI) was largely an attempt to recreate the flow of conversation that occurs naturally between student and tutor. But CAI has not yet become a mainstay of the educational process, for several reasons.

First, the most sophisticated instructional software cannot be as flexible or as creative as a human tutor, and consequently it cannot duplicate the controlled but relatively free flow of private instruction. Second, although students show no signs of resenting certain kinds of instruction by machine, they do resent contrived interaction with the computer. Third, even with the best computer-assisted instruction, students nearly always seek interaction with their instructor, if only to point out their accomplishments; human-to-human dialogue seems to be an essential ingredient *at some point* in the learning process. Fourth, there has been a lack of good CAI materials, the development of which is a long and costly process. Fifth, CAI has been a very expensive form of instruction and therefore a difficult one to finance at the local level.

Nevertheless, there has been widespread use of CAI in a specific environment—urban districts with large numbers of underachieving students. Great strides have been made using CAI with these students, and federal money has been available in support of this type of program. We believe that considerable benefit is to be gained from a selective use of CAI at all levels of education, with the right mode of instruction, the right target group of students, and the right mix of student-teacher-machine interaction.

The complexity of the CAI curriculum that can be implemented at your school is limited by your computer resources: the memory size, the amount of mass storage available, the speed of access, and the type of display. Let's look at several levels of machine sophistication and the type of CAI feasible for each.

On our Commodore PET, for instance, we are quite limited. With only 8 k of RAM and a (slow) cassette tape drive, we can't execute very large programs; nor can we read different programs in and out of memory very quickly. Yet we can offer drill-and-practice on arithmetic facts, foreign language vocabulary quizzes, and science and social science review tutorials.

A large computer, with perhaps 32 k of RAM and a disk drive, could be used to conduct a one-year review course on basic arithmetic, to maintain performance and statistics files for teacher use, or to present a unit on the Civil War with lessons on the battles and on the economic factors involved in the war.

A more sophisticated computer—with even more memory, dual disk drives, time-sharing and possibly a special-purpose language for authoring CAI—would allow a school-wide program with multiple terminals simultaneously interacting with the same or different materials. In this environment, you could supply complete courses in as many subjects as are offered, with extensive group and individual record-keeping.

Each level of machine sophistication is of course more costly, but a microcomputer-based program is significantly cheaper than any of the others. About the cheapest CAI cost before 1975 was $1 per student hour; with the PET, at least some phases of the same program can be delivered for about 11 cents per student hour. At the present time, we would not advocate replacement of an existing CAI system with a low end microcomputer-based system; the same quality of instruction could probably not be achieved immediately. But the school that has been wanting to dabble in CAI for some special purpose, along with miscellaneous other computer activities, can finally try it at a reasonable cost.

An Overview of CAI

Let's back up for a moment to discuss CAI in general—what it is, what it offers, how it is used, and how well it works.

What Is It?

CAI is a method of instruction by which the computer actually teaches the student. The two main modes of CAI are *drill and practice*, designed to assist the student in maintaining and mastering a skill, and *tutorial*, designed to assist the student in acquiring a skill.

For example, a drill and practice program on plurals of words assumes that the student has learned the applicable rule but needs practice in applying it. The drill might go as follows:

WHAT IS THE PLURAL OF SKY? *SKYS*
NO, TRY AGAIN. WHAT IS THE PLURAL OF SKY? *SKIES*
THAT'S RIGHT!
WHAT IS THE PLURAL OF TRY? *TRIES*
THAT'S RIGHT! HERE'S THE LAST ONE.
WHAT IS THE PLURAL OF FLY? *FLIES*
GOOD! YOU GOT 2 OUT OF 3 CORRECT. JUST REMEMBER,
WORDS THAT END IN Y USUALLY FORM THEIR PLURAL
BY CHANGING THE Y TO I AND ADDING ES.

On the other hand, a tutorial on the same subject would first present the rule, then respond to incorrect answers by pointing out the error before asking the student to try again:

WORDS THAT END IN Y GENERALLY FORM THEIR
PLURAL BY CHANGING THE Y TO I AND ADDING ES.
THUS TRY BECOMES TRIES, PRY BECOMES PRIES, AND
SO ON.
WHY DON'T YOU TRY ONE?
WHAT IS THE PLURAL OF SKY? *SKYS*
NO, REMEMBER THE RULE ABOUT WORDS THAT END IN
Y. NOW, WHAT IS THE PLURAL OF SKY? *SKES*
NO, YOU HAVE THE IDEA BUT YOU MISSPELLED THE
ANSWER.
TRY AGAIN. WHAT IS THE PLURAL OF SKY? *SKIES*
THERE, YOU GOT IT! HERE'S ANOTHER ONE:

.

.

.

and so on.

We feel that drill and practice is the most effective mode of computer-assisted instruction. Humans seem to be unnecessary when the goal is simply practice and more practice. The important thing is that the drill is delivered quickly with a minimum of waiting, which is, of course, the computer's forte. Also, an element of competition usually develops—student versus machine—that eliminates some of the tedium of the repetitive drill.

Tutorial CAI is an important secondary mode. It is particularly useful for make-up lessons for absentees and for students working individually, perhaps on advanced placement work.

What Does CAI Offer?

Numerous benefits are to be gained from a CAI program—and they apply to both students and teachers, making school a more successful and enjoyable experience for both. These benefits are similar to the general good derived from computer use in general, as discussed in Chapter 2.

1. *CAI provides individualized, self-paced instruction.* Within a particular unit or course, students move as quickly or as slowly as they want. In a complex curriculum, the student is routed to review or enrichment lessons based on performance on the core materials.

2. *CAI can significantly upgrade student performance.* Impressive gains have been found both in the cognitive and affective domains after a period of regular work with the CAI program. Underachieving groups have actually surpassed the performance of average and above-average students in some cases.

3. *CAI can be highly motivating even to students caught in the vicious cycle of underachievement.* The novelty of the computer usually catches the interest of these students. From that point, the unhurried pace of the instruction—with no criticism of errors beyond "Sorry, try again"— generally maintains it. The whole process can be very motivating to students who have been at the bottom of the heap from the time they entered school.

4. *CAI can allow an increase in student/teacher ratio without the students' performance being adversely affected.* When the computer assumes the burden of providing drill and practice, make-up lessons, and reviews, the teacher can interact effectively in other areas with a greater number of students.

5. *CAI can help teachers to better diagnose areas of student weakness.* A good CAI program, with carefully chosen objectives and test questions and with a good record-keeping system, can help teachers more accurately pinpoint the areas in which students need work. Also, the students advance through the material as quickly as they master each objective. Teachers can quickly ascertain the exact position of each student in the curriculum.

6. *CAI can cause a shift in the role of the teacher—from adversary to ally.* In the traditional classroom, the teacher is The Enemy, handing out assignments, criticizing, and judging. But in the CAI classroom, the teacher's role is more that of coach, encouraging students and giving them hints on how to master the material.

7. *CAI ensures the application of proven teaching methods to all students at all times.* A computer never gets tired or impatient, and it can't discriminate even unconsciously because of a student's personality or background. It repeats a question or lesson as many times as necessary, and it waits as long as scheduled for the student response.

8. *CAI provides immediate feedback to the student.* The most effective instruction follows each question-response pair with an immediate "right" or "wrong." The student is able to correct the mistake immediately, without any ensuing period of confusion.

How Is CAI Used?

As noted above, CAI is used mostly to upgrade the performance of underachieving students. It isn't clear why programs have not evolved for average and above-average students, but the lack is probably tied to the availability of funds for compensatory education programs. Consequently, we have seen CAI programs in urban areas with a high number of educationally disadvantaged youngsters, in special programs for the physically and mentally handicapped, and in remedial programs in secondary schools and higher education. But we see nothing to prevent just as effective an application of CAI to the average and gifted students in our schools.

How Well Does CAI Work?

Numerous studies have shown that CAI can be tremendously effective, especially with the slower student groups. Students at the elementary level who were two years or more below grade level in mathematics have gained up to 1.35 years after one year in a program consisting of ten minutes per day of interaction with a well-known computer-assisted mathematics package.* Also, significant gains in attendance have been reported when CAI programs are in use.**

Back to Micro CAI

Having answered these fundamental questions, let's look at some typical CAI applications that might be implemented on a microcomputer.

Math

There are a number of applications in mathematics, the simplest of which is random drill in arithmetic facts. The most rudimentary form of arithmetic drill can be done with just a few lines of code, producing the following results:

*Dr. Arthur L. Maser, and Vernon Johnson, "Highline School District," *Hewlett-Packard Educational Users Group Newsletter* (May/June 1977).

**"D.C. Secondary Schools Project for Computer-Aided Education," *Hewlett-Packard Educational Users Group Newsletter* (May/June 1977).

$5 + 3 = 6$
WRONG, TRY AGAIN
$5 + 3 = 8$
$6 + 2 = 7$
WRONG, TRY AGAIN
$6 + 2 = 8$
$1 + 4 = 5$
and so on.

The code takes just seven lines:

```
READY.
  10 X=INT(RND(TI)*10)
  20 Y=INT(RND(TI)*10)
  30 PRINT X"+"Y"=";
  40 INPUT Z
  50 IF Z=X+Y THEN 10
  60 PRINT "WRONG, TRY AGAIN."
  70 GOTO 30
READY.
```

Once you run this program, however, you find that there are several things that would be nice to include. For instance, you would like to be able to specify the number of problems, keep track of how many the student has answered correctly, tell the student the answer if he or she misses a certain number of tries, and address the student by name. None of these features is difficult to include—each just requires additional lines of code. The sample run and program for this more sophisticated drill are as follows:

HI. WHAT IS YOUR NAME? *CHRIS*
OKAY, CHRIS, HERE ARE SOME
ADDITION PROBLEMS.
$2 + 3 = ?$ *5*
$3 + 4 = ?$ *6*
NO, TRY THAT ONE AGAIN.
$3 + 4 = ?$ *7*
$2 + 5 = ?$ *7*
$1 + 4 = ?$ *5*
$7 + 6 = ?$ *11*
NOPE, TRY THAT ONE AGAIN.
$7 + 6 = ?$ *13*
GOOD, CHRIS, YOU GOT 3 OUT
OF 5 CORRECT.
DO YOU WANT MORE (1 = YES 0 = NO)? *0*
READY.

The code for this drill is only slightly more complicated than the previous program, though it is longer. C is the count of the number of problems (5), T is the number of tries (maximum of 3) for any one problem, and G is the number of times the student answers a problem correctly the first time (or when T = 1). The program is:

```
READY.
          10 INPUT "HI. WHAT IS YOUR NAME";A$
          20 PRINT "OKAY,"A$" ,HERE ARE SOME "
          21 PRINT "ADDITION PROBLEMS."
          30 C=C+1
          40 IF C>5 THEN 190
          50 T=1
          60 X=INT(RND(TI)*10)
          70 Y=INT(RND(TI)*10)
          80 PRINT X"+"Y"=";
          90 INPUT Z
          100 IF Z<>X+Y THEN 124
          110 IF T=1 THEN G=G+1
          120 GOTO 30
          124 T=T+1
          126 IF T>3 THEN 160
          130 PRINT "NOPE,TRY THAT ONE AGAIN."
          150 GOTO 80
          160 PRINT "SORRY, THE ANSWER IS "X+Y
          180 GOTO 30
          190 PRINT "GOOD,"A$" ,YOU GOT "G"OUT"
          191 PRINT "OF 5 CORRECT."
          200 INPUT "DO YOU WANT MORE (1=YES 0=NO)";B
          210 IF B=1 THEN C=0:T=0:G=0:GOTO 30
          220 END
READY.
```

The program can be easily modified to be more flexible. For instance, changing statements 60 and 70 changes the range of the addend and augend. You can easily change the number of problems or the number of tries allowed by simply changing the maximum value of C in statements 40 and 191 or of T in statement 126.

```
READY.
          10 INPUT "HI. WHAT IS YOUR NAME";A$
          20 PRINT "OKAY,"A$" ,HERE ARE SOME "
          21 PRINT "ADDITION PROBLEMS."
          30 C=C+1
          40 IF C>5 THEN 190
          50 T=1
          60 X=INT(RND(TI)*20)
          70 Y=INT(RND(TI)*20)
          80 PRINT X"+"Y"=";
          90 INPUT Z
          100 IF Z<>X+Y THEN 124
          110 IF T=1 THEN G=G+1
          120 GOTO 30
          124 T=T+1
          126 IF T>3 THEN 160
          130 PRINT "NOPE,TRY THAT ONE AGAIN."
```

```
150 GOTO 80
160 PRINT "SORRY, THE ANSWER IS "X+Y
180 GOTO 30
190 PRINT "GOOD,"A$" ,YOU GOT "G"OUT"
191 PRINT "OF 5 CORRECT."
200 INPUT "DO YOU WANT MORE (1=YES 0=NO)";B
210 IF B=1 THEN C=0:T=0:G=0:GOTO 30
220 END
READY.
```

The only change required for multiplication is to change the operand " + " to "*" in statements 80, 100, and 160 and to replace the word "ADDITION" with "MULTIPLICATION" in statement 21. Subtraction and division are a little trickier if you want only combinations that yield positive integers as a result. Subtraction also requires a test to see if X and Y must be switched so that X − Y will be non-negative. Changes to the program would look like this:

```
 21 PRINT "SUBTRACTION PROBLEMS."
 71 IF X >= Y THEN 80
 72 H = X:X = Y:Y = H
 80 PRINT X; "-"; Y; " =";
100 IF Z<> X − Y THEN 124
160 PRINT "SORRY, THE ANSWER IS "; X − Y$
```

Division requires multiplying X by Y to get the dividend of the division problem. Thus, since X is the divisor, it must be checked for 0 and regenerated if it is 0. Changes to the same original program are:

```
 21 PRINT "DIVISION PROBLEMS."
 71  IF X = 0 THEN 60
 75 W = X*Y
 80 PRINT W; "/";X;" =";
100 IF Z <> Y THEN 124
160 PRINT "SORRY, THE ANSWER IS "; Y
```

Another possibility is to drill students on a particular addition or multiplication table. This too is easy to do:

```
READY.

10 INPUT "HI. WHAT IS YOUR NAME";A$
15 PRINT "WHAT NUMBER DO YOU WISH TO"
16 INPUT "PRACTICE ADDING";X
20 PRINT "OKAY,"A$" ,HERE ARE SOME "
21 PRINT "ADDITION PROBLEMS."
30 C=C+1
```

```
40 IF C>5 THEN 190
50 T=1
70 Y=INT(RND(TI)*10)
80 PRINT X"+"Y"=";
90 INPUT Z
100 IF Z<>X+Y THEN 124
110 IF T=1 THEN G=G+1
120 GOTO 30
124 T=T+1
126 IF T>3 THEN 160
130 PRINT "NOPE,TRY THAT ONE AGAIN."
150 GOTO 80
160 PRINT "SORRY, THE ANSWER IS "X+Y
180 GOTO 30
190 PRINT "GOOD,"A$" ,YOU GOT "G"OUT"
191 PRINT "OF 5 CORRECT."
200 INPUT "DO YOU WANT MORE (1=YES 0=NO)";B
210 IF B=1 THEN C=0:T=0:G=0:GOTO 30
220 END
READY.
```

The nicest program, of course, allows the student to choose not only the skill he or she wishes to practice but also the range of numbers to be included in the problems. This selectivity can be achieved in one main program with four subsections for the four skills (addition, subtraction, multiplication, and division), with control passing to the main program at the end of each group of problems so the student can choose to practice a different skill if he or she wishes.

The following program shows how this is done in the most straightforward manner, with each subsection containing all the code necessary to generate problems in that skill area. Only the addition subsection is shown, to illustrate the technique. (A more efficient method for accomplishing the same task will be shown, but the programming will be a little more complicated.) The main routine (lines 10-110) is straightforward and shows that the addition routine starts at 1000, subtraction at 2000, and so on. The logic in the addition routine from 1110 to 1225 is easily followed since it is very close to our earlier arithmetic program. Lines 1010 to 1100 set up the parameters M and Q, which generate the requested number of digits in lines 1120 and 1130. Lines 1226 and 1228 check the mastery of the skill.

```
READY.

10 PRINT "HELLO,WHAT'S YOUR NAME";
20 INPUT A$
30 PRINT "WELL "A$", I AM HERE TO DRILL"
40 PRINT "YOU ON YOUR ARITHMETIC FACTS."
50 PRINT "WHICH SKILL DO YOU WISH TO PRACTICE?"
60 PRINT "   A=ADDITION"
61 PRINT "   S=SUBTRACTION"
62 PRINT "   M=MULTIPLICATION"
63 PRINT "   D=DIVISION"
64 PRINT "   0=STOP"
70 INPUT S$
80 IF S$="A" THEN 1000
85 IF S$="S" THEN 2000
90 IF S$="M" THEN 3000
95 IF S$="D" THEN 4000
100 IF S$="0" THEN 9999
```

```
110 GOTO 50
1000 REM   ADDITION SUBROUTINE
1010 PRINT "DO YOU WANT TO ADD 1,2,OR"
1011 PRINT "3 DIGIT NUMBERS";
1020 INPUT N
1040 IF N=3 THEN 1100
1050 IF N=2 THEN 1080
1055 IF N<>1 THEN 1010
1060 M=10:Q=0
1070 GOTO 1110
1080 M=90:Q=10
1090 GOTO 1110
1100 M=900:Q=100
1110 INPUT "HOW MANY PROBLEMS";P
1115 FOR I=1 TO P
1120 X=INT(RND(TI)*M)+Q
1130 Y=INT(RND(TI)*M)+Q
1135 T=1
1140 PRINT X"+"Y"=";
1150 INPUT Z
1160 IF Z=X+Y THEN 1210
1170 T=T+1
1180 IF T>3 THEN PRINT "NO,"X"+"Y"="X+Y :GOTO 1220
1190 PRINT "NO, TRY AGAIN."
1200 GOTO 1140
1210 IF T=1 THEN G=G+1
1220 NEXT I
1225 PRINT "YOU GOT "G" OUT OF "P" CORRECT."
1227 G=0
1230 GOTO 50
2000 REM SUBTRACTION SUBROUTINE
    .
    .
    .
```

To this program, you would add other routines starting at 2000 for subtraction, 3000 for multiplication, and so on. The more efficient method presented in the next program is fully expanded for all four skills. This method takes advantage of the portions of code that are common to all four skills by placing those portions in the main routine. Thus, lines 10–110 are very similar to the previous version, but lines 120–350 represent the common portions added to the main routine. Lines 150–180 cause control to pass to the proper routine to generate the problem for that skill. The variable 0$ is the operator for the current skill: $+$, $-$, $*$, or $/$. Each routine (starting at 1000, 2000, 3000, or 4000) does the set-up work to accomplish the corresponding skill by defining M, Q, and 0$. Each routine (starting at 1500, 3500, or 4500) generates the problem by defining X, Y, and A (the expected answer), with 1500 doubling for addition and subtraction.

```
READY.

10 PRINT "HELLO,WHAT'S YOUR NAME";
20 INPUT A$
30 PRINT "WELL "A$", I AM HERE TO DRILL"
40 PRINT "YOU ON YOUR ARITHMETIC FACTS."
50 PRINT "WHICH SKILL DO YOU WISH TO PRACTICE?"
60 PRINT "  A=ADDITION"
61 PRINT "  S=SUBTRACTION"
62 PRINT "  M=MULTIPLICATION"
63 PRINT "  D=DIVISION"
64 PRINT "  0=STOP"
70 INPUT S$
```

```
80 IF S$="A" THEN 1000
85 IF S$="S" THEN 2000
90 IF S$="M" THEN 3000
95 IF S$="D" THEN 4000
100 IF S$="0" THEN 9999
110 GOTO 50
120 INPUT "HOW MANY PROBLEMS";P
130 IF P<1 THEN 120
140 FOR I=1 TO P
150 IF S$="A" THEN 1500
160 IF S$="S" THEN 1500
170 IF S$="M" THEN 3500
180 GOTO 4500
190 T=1
200 PRINT X;O$;Y;"=";
210 INPUT Z
220 IF Z=A THEN 270
230 T=T+1
240 IF T>3 THEN PRINT "NO,";X;O$;Y;"=";A: GOTO 280
250 PRINT "NO, TRY AGAIN"
260 GOTO200
270 IF T=1 THEN G=G+1
280 NEXT I
290 PRINT "YOU GOT";G;"OUT OF";P;"CORRECT."
300 IF G/P>.9 THEN PRINT "THAT'S GOOD.":GOTO 330
310 IF G/P>.74 THEN PRINT "NOT BAD, BUT YOU NEED MORE PRACTICE":GOTO 330
320 PRINT "I THINK YOU NEED MORE WORK ON THIS  SKILL, OR EASIER PROBLEMS."
330 G=0
340 PRINT
350 GOTO 50
1000 REM ADDITION SETUP ROUTINE
1010 PRINT "DO YOU WANT TO ADD 1,2,OR"
1011 PRINT "3 DIGIT NUMBERS";
1020 INPUT N
1040 IF N=3 THEN 1100
1050 IF N=2 THEN 1080
1055 IF N<>1 THEN 1010
1060 M=10:Q=0
1070 GOTO 1110
1080 M=90:Q=10
1090 GOTO 1110
1100 M=900:Q=100
1110 O$="+"
1120 IF S$="S" THEN O$="-"
1130 GOTO 120
1500 REM ADDITION AND SUBTRACTION PROBLEM GENERATION ROUTINE
1510 X=INT(RND(TI)*M)+Q
1520 Y=INT(RND(TI)*M)+Q
1530 A=X+Y
1540 IF S$="A" THEN 190
1550 IF X<Y THEN H=X:X=Y:Y=H
1560 A=X-Y
1570 GOTO 190
2000 REM SUBRACTION SETUP ROUTINE
2010 PRINT "DO YOU WANT TO SUBTRACT 1,2, OR"
2020 GOTO 1011
3000 REM MULTIPLICATION SETUP ROUTINE
3010 O$="*"
3020 PRINT "YOU WILL BE MULTIPLYING A 1-DIGIT"
3030 PRINT "NUMBER BY A 1-DIGIT OR A 2-DIGIT"
3040 PRINT "NUMBER."
3050 INPUT "WHICH DO YOU WANT (1 OR 2)";N
3060 IF N=1 THEN M=10: Q=0: GOTO 120
3070 IF N<>2 THEN 3050
3080 M=90: Q=10
3090 GOTO 120
3500 REM MULTIPLICATION PROBLEM GENERATION ROUTINE
3510 X=INT(RND(TI)*M)+Q
```

```
3520 Y=INT(RND(TI)*10)
3530 A=X*Y
3540 GOTO 190
4000 REM DIVISION SETUP ROUTINE
4010 PRINT "YOU WILL BE DIVIDING A NUMBER BY"
4020 PRINT "ANOTHER NUMBER WHICH WILL BE 1 OR 2"
4030 PRINT "DIGITS."
4040 O$="/"
4050 GOTO 3050
4500 REM DIVISION PROBLEM GENERATION ROUTINE
4510 A=INT(RND(TI)*10)
4520 Y=INT(RND(TI)*M)+Q
4530 IF Y=0 THEN 4520
4540 X=A*Y
4550 GOTO 190
9999 END
READY.
```

Languages

Foreign language instruction is another obvious application of CAI. Students can be drilled on vocabulary, verb conjugations, sentence structure, and other fundamentals. Examples with verb conjugations and with vocabulary are shown in the following program (as with the arithmetic drill, a simple version is shown first):

> BONJOUR. COMMENT VOUS APPELEZ-VOUS? *JEANINE*
> BIEN, JEANINE, VOULEZ-VOUS CONTINUER?
> (1 = OUI 0 = NON)?*1*
> AUJOURD'HUI NOUS ALLONS PRATIQUER LA
> VERBE ETRE. COMPLETEZ LES PHRASES
> SUIVANTES.
> JE? *SUIS*
> TU? *ES*
> IL/ELLE? *EST*
> NOUS? *AVONS*
> NON, ESSAYEZ ENCORE.
> NOUS? *SOMMES*
> VOUS? *ETES*
> ILS/ELLES? *SONT*

The code for this exercise is quite simple. After going through the sequence shown in the sample RUN, it cycles through the pronouns again backwards, to provide extra practice.

```
READY.
10 PRINT"BONJOUR. COMMENT VOUS APPELEZ-VOUS?"
20 INPUT N$
30 PRINT"BIEN ";N$;",VOULEZ-VOUS CONTINUER"
40 INPUT "(1=OUI 0=NON)";A
50 IF A<>1 THEN END
```

```
60 FOR I=0 TO 6
70 READ V$(I)
80 NEXT I
82 FOR I=1 TO 6
83 READ P$(I)
84 NEXT I
86 PRINT
90 PRINT"AUJOURD'HUI NOUS ALLONS PRATIQUER LA"
100 PRINT" VERBE ";V$(O);". COMPLETEZ LES PHRASES "
105 PRINT"SUIVANTES."
106 PRINT
110 FOR I=1 TO 6
120 PRINT P$(I);:INPUT A$
130 IF A$=V$(I) THEN 160
140 PRINT "NON, ESSAYEZ ENCORE."
150 GOTO 120
160 NEXT I
170 FOR I=5 TO 1 STEP -1
180 PRINT P$(I);:INPUT A$(I)
190 IF A$(I)=V$(I) THEN 220
200 PRINT "NON, ESSAYEZ ENCORE."
210 GOTO 180
220 NEXT I
300 DATA ETRE,SUIS,ES,EST,SOMMES,ETES,SONT
310 DATA JE,TU,IL/ELLE,NOUS,VOUS,ILS/ELLES
400 END
READY.
```

A similar drill can be done for a list of vocabulary words, first giving French and asking for the English equivalent, and then vice versa.

BONJOUR.
HERE IS A FRENCH VOCABULARY QUIZ.
I WILL GIVE YOU TEN FRENCH WORDS, ONE AT A TIME.
GIVE ME THE ENGLISH EQUIVALENT.
LA FLEUR? *FLOWER*
L'ARBRE? *TREE*
LE TAPIS? *TAPESTRY*
NO, THE ANSWER IS CARPET.
LA MAIN? *HAND*
LE PAPIER? *PAPER*
LE FROMAGE? *CHEESE*
NOW, LET'S TRY ANOTHER WAY.
I'LL GIVE YOU ENGLISH, YOU GIVE ME FRENCH.
WINDOW? *LA FENETRE*

.
.
.

Here is the program:

```
10 PRINT"BONJOUR."
15 PRINT
20 PRINT"HERE IS A FRENCH VOCABULARY QUIZ."
30 PRINT"I WILL GIVE YOU TEN FRENCH WORDS, ONE AT A TIME."
40 PRINT"GIVE ME THE ENGLISH EQUIVALENT."
45 PRINT
```

```
50 FOR I=1 TO10
60 READ F$(I)
70 NEXT I
80 FOR I=1 TO 10
90 READ E$(I)
100 NEXT I
105 FOR I=1 TO10
110 PRINT F$(I);:INPUT A$(I)
120 IF A$(I)=E$(I) THEN 140
130 PRINT "NO, THE ANSWER IS ";E$(I)
140 NEXT I
150 PRINT "NOW, LET'S TRY ANOTHER WAY."
160 PRINT "I'LL GIVE YOU ENGLISH YOU GIVE ME FRENCH."
170 FOR I=10 TO 1 STEP -1
180 PRINT E$(I);:INPUT A$(I)
190 IF A$(I)=F$(I) THEN 210
200 PRINT "NO, THE ANSWER IS ";F$(I)
210 NEXT I
220 PRINT "THAT'S ALL. SEE YOU LATER."
300 DATA L'ARBRE,LE TABLE,LA MAIN,LES VETEMENTS,LE STYLO,LE PAPIER,LE FROMAGE
310 DATA LA FLEUR,LE TAPIS,LA FENETRE
320 DATA TREE,TABLE,HAND,CLOTHES,PEN,PAPER
330 DATA CHEESE,FLOWER,CARPET,WINDOW
400 END
```

Other Disciplines

The subjects of history and chemistry provide a good opportunity for tutorial CAI—for students making up a class, reviewing for a test, or doing individual work. The following example shows a very straightforward approach:

HELLO, WHAT IS YOUR NAME? *CHRIS*
CHRIS, TODAY WE ARE GOING TO TALK ABOUT THE
FIRST THREE PRESIDENTS OF THE UNITED STATES. OF
COURSE, YOU KNOW WHO THE FIRST PRESIDENT
WAS, DON'T YOU, CHRIS? *YES*
TELL ME HIS LAST NAME? *WASHINGTON*
THAT'S RIGHT. IN 1789, GEORGE WASHINGTON
WAS ELECTED PRESIDENT BY A UNANIMOUS VOTE OF
THE STATE ELECTORS. JOHN ADAMS WAS HIS VICE-
PRESIDENT FOR BOTH TERMS (1789–1796).

(The text continues with a discussion of the next two elections, party politics in those days, and the passage of the Twelfth Amendment.)

Once the text has been presented, the student should be quizzed on the details within it:

OK CHRIS, NOW I'M GOING TO ASK YOU SOME
QUESTIONS.

A. WHO WAS ELECTED PRESIDENT IN 1796?
   1. GEORGE WASHINGTON
   2. JOHN ADAMS
   3. ABRAHAM LINCOLN
TYPE THE NUMBER OF THE CORRECT ANSWER
?3

NO, LINCOLN WAS PRESIDENT FROM 1860–1865. TRY AGAIN.
?1

NO, WASHINGTON DECLINED NOMINATION FOR A THIRD TERM.
THE ANSWER IS JOHN ADAMS
B. WHO WAS JOHN ADAMS' VICE-PRESIDENT?
   1. AARON BURR
   2. JOHN QUINCY ADAMS
   3. THOMAS JEFFERSON
   .
   .
   .

etc.

The program that produces this output is relatively simple:

```
READY.

10 PRINT "HELLO, WHAT IS YOUR NAME";:INPUT N$
15 PRINT
20 PRINT N$;",TODAY WE ARE GOING TO TALK ABOUT"
30 PRINT " THE FIRST THREE PRESIDENTS OF THE "
40 PRINT "UNITED STATES.  OF COURSE, YOU KNOW "
50 PRINT "WHO THE FIRST PRESIDENT WAS, DON'T YOU "
60 PRINT "CHRIS";
70 INPUT A$
80 IF A$="NO" THEN 110
90 PRINT "TELL ME HIS LAST NAME";:INPUT A$
100 IF A$="WASHINGTON" THEN 119
105 PRINT
110 PRINT "I'LL TELL YOU. IT WAS WASHINGTON."
119 PRINT
120 PRINT "GEORGE WASHINGTON WAS ELECTED IN "
130 PRINT "1789 BY A UNANIMOUS VOTE OF THE "
140 PRINT "STATE ELECTORS. JOHN ADAMS WAS HIS "
150 PRINT "VICE PRESIDENT FOR HIS TWO TERMS "
155 PRINT
160 PRINT "(1789-1796)."
165 PRINT
1000 PRINT "OK,";N$;", I'M GOING TO ASK YOU SOME QUESTIONS."
1005 PRINT
1010 PRINT "A. WHO WAS ELECTED PRESIDENT IN 1796 "
1020 PRINT "  1. GEORGE WASHINGTON"
1030 PRINT "  2. JOHN ADAMS"
1040 PRINT "  3. ABRAHAM LINCOLN"
1050 PRINT "TYPE THE NUMBER OF THE CORRECT ANSWER"
1060 INPUT A
```

```
1070 IF A=1 THEN PRINT "THAT'S RIGHT.":GOTO 1155
1080 IF A=2 THEN 1110
1090 IF A=3 THEN 1130
1100 PRINT "PLEASE,";N$;:GOTO 1050
1110 PRINT "NO, ADAMS WAS ELECTED VICE-PRESIDENT IN 1796."
1120 GOTO 1140
1130 PRINT "NO, LINCOLN WAS PRESIDENT FROM 1860-1865."
1140 PRINT "TRY AGAIN.":GOTO 1060
1150 PRINT
1155 PRINT
1160 PRINT "B. WHO WAS JOHN ADAMS' VICE-PRESIDENT"
1170 PRINT" 1. AARON BURR"
1180 PRINT" 2. JOHN QUINCY ADAMS"
1190 PRINT" 3. THOMAS JEFFERSON  "
2000 END
READY.
```

There are two problems with preparing lessons of this sort, one inevitable and the other potentially solvable. First, lessons with a lot of text consume a lot of memory space—this tiny portion of a lesson used 1,227 bytes of storage. Second, programming lessons with a lot of text is pretty boring; eventually when a variety of authoring languages are available, this task will be less tedious. An authoring language generally allows you to enter lesson material directly, with simple procedures for jumping and looping. Special statements are used to indicate questions, correct answers, incorrect answers, coded responses to the student, and so forth. In other words, an authoring language eliminates most of the programming aspects of lesson development—"all" you have to do is design the lesson itself. As software is developed for microcomputers, these languages will become available.

One such language, PILOT, has already been implemented for most 8 k BASIC systems. To write a PILOT program, you simply type a one-letter code for one of thirteen possible statement types you are using, and then you input your lesson material. For instance:

```
10 T: HELLO! WHAT IS YOUR NAME +
20 A: $ NAME
30 T: WELL $NAME, TODAY YOU WILL BE TESTED ON THE
40 T: FIRST THREE PRESIDENTS OF THE UNITED STATES +
50 T: WHO WAS THE FIRST PRESIDENT OF THE U.S. +
60 A:
70 M: WASHINGTON, GEORGE WASHINGTON
80 Y: THAT'S RIGHT!
90 JY: *QUESTION2
100 T: NO, GEORGE WASHINGTON WAS THE FIRST
PRESIDENT.
```

110 *QUESTION2 T: WHO WAS ELECTED PRESIDENT IN 1796+

.
.
.

etc.

This language is certainly easier and faster to use than BASIC. Further-more, it offers more flexibility; for example, you can match for both WASHINGTON and GEORGE WASHINGTON in line 70.

Review Exercises

Another approach to CAI is to use the computer for review before a test. For example, you could present the student with a practice quiz of ten questions drawn at random from a bank of test items, as shown in this example from a chemistry course:

HELLO. WHAT'S YOUR NAME? *CHRIS*
OK, CHRIS. I WILL GIVE YOU A FEW QUESTIONS LIKE
THOSE YOU WILL FIND ON THE TEST TOMORROW.
WHAT IS THE CHEMICAL SYMBOL FOR THE FOLLOWING
ELEMENTS? (FOR EXAMPLE, OXYGEN IS O)
    OXYGEN? *O*
    HYDROGEN? *H*
    NITROGEN? *N*
GOOD. NOW HERE ARE A COUPLE OF TRICKY ONES.
    CHLORINE? *Cl*
    MAGNESIUM? *Mg*   Note: This would be the RUN
    SODIUM? *So*   only if you have an upper *and*
    NO, TRY AGAIN   lower case terminal.
    SODIUM? *Na*
    IRON? *Fe*
GOOD JOB. BE SURE TO REVIEW ALL THE CHEMICAL
SYMBOLS.
NOW TELL ME THE NAMES OF THE FOLLOWING
RADICALS.
    OH? *HYDROXIDE*
.
.
.

etc.

Program.

```
READY.

 1 REM *** CHEM REVIEW PROGRAM ***
 5 REM *** CHEM REVIEW PROGRAM ***
10 DIM E$(16),S$(16)
12 REM  E$= TABLE OF ELEMENTS
13 REM  S$= TABLE OF SYMBOLS
15 FOR I=1 TO 16
20 READ E$(I),S$(I)
25 NEXT I
30 PRINT "HELLO. WHAT IS YOUR NAME";
35 INPUT B$
40 PRINT "OK,";B$;". I WILL GIVE YOU A FEW QUESTIONS ";
45 PRINT "LIKE YOU WILL FIND ON THE NEXT TEST."
50 PRINT
55 PRINT "WHAT IS THE CHEMICAL SYMBOL FOR THE"
60 PRINT "FOLLOWING ELEMENTS (E.G., OXYGEN IS O)"
69 REM  Z=NUMBER OF TRIES
70 FOR I=1 TO 3
72 REM  Z=NUMBER OF TRIES
75 Z=0
80 X=INT(RND(TI)*10)+1
85 PRINT E$(X);
90 INPUT A$
95 IF A$=S$(X) THEN 125
96 IF Z=0 THEN C=C+1
100 Z=Z+1
105 IF Z>=3 THEN 120
110 PRINT "NO, TRY AGAIN."
115 GOTO 85
120 PRINT "NO, THE SYMBOL IS ";S$(X)
122 IF I<3 THEN PRINT "TRY ANOTHER."
125 NEXT I
135 IF C>1 THEN PRINT B$;",YOU NEED MORE STUDY BEFORE TOMORROW."
140 PRINT "NOW HERE ARE A COUPLE OF TRICKY ONES."
145 FOR I=1 TO 3
150 Z=0
155 X=INT(RND(TI)*6)+11
160 PRINT E$(X)
165 INPUT A$
170 IF A$=S$(X) THEN 200
171 IF Z=0 THEN C=C+1
175 Z=Z+1
180 IF Z>=3 THEN 195
185 PRINT "NO,TRY AGAIN."
190 GOTO 160
195 PRINT "NO, THE SYMBOL IS ";S$(X)
198 IF I<3 THEN PRINT "TRY ANOTHER!"
200 NEXT I
210 IF C>2 THEN PRINT B$;", YOU SHOULD STUDY THESE SYMBOLS BEFORE THE TEST."
215 PRINT
220 PRINT "OK, TELL ME THE NAMES OF THE FOLLOWING"
225 PRINT "RADICALS..."
230 DATA OXYGEN,O,HYDROGEN,H,CARBON,C
231 DATA NITROGEN,N,FLUORINE,F,BORON,B
232 DATA PHOSPHORUS,P,SULFUR,S,POTACLOSESSIUM,K
233 DATA CHLORINE,CL,MAGNESIUM,MG,SODIUM,NA
234 DATA IRON,FE,CALCIUM,CA,SILVER,AG,ZINC,ZN
READY.
 1380

READY.
```

Picking the test items at random from the arrays makes it possible for the student to take a review quiz, determine weak points, study in those areas, and return to take a similar test with at least some different elements.

And So It Goes ...

By now, you should begin to see the potential for CAI even on a small machine like the PET. None of these programs even approached capacity of our system, and each took only a short while to program.

In a more sophisticated development environment, a support mechanism would surely be provided for record-keeping, conditional branching from lesson to lesson, large item banks for test generation, and more extensive answer processing. But the student materials don't change a great deal from those provided here.

We don't represent these programs as examples of exceptionally good instructional design, and we urge you to study some of the references at the end of this chapter before attempting any major curriculum development. For anything more extensive than simple drills and tutorials, such as those shown in this chapter, we recommend a team approach with both subject matter specialists and experienced instructional programmers. But we do believe that the application of simple, special-purpose CAI lessons has its place in many a classroom, especially in districts that cannot offer a carefully designed and developed CAI curriculum.

There is a recommended cycle for CAI development, with two very important steps that are too often overlooked—*field testing* and *modification*. The best CAI materials have been through several rounds of testing and modification to sharpen the focus and straighten out any unanticipated problems. The figure most often quoted as the ratio of development hours to student hours is 200:1 (that is, 200 hours of development to produce a program that a student uses for 1 hour)—not very encouraging to the average teacher. This ratio includes instructional design as well as lesson preparation, programming, testing, and modification. What we have tried to show in this chapter is the much better ratio that can be gained from a compromise commitment by individual teachers who want to use CAI to reinforce or assist their efforts in specific ways well known to them.

References

Anastasio, Ernest J., "Computer-Based Education: Obstacles to Its Use and Plans for Future Action," *Viewpoints* (July 1974).
Bell, Frederick H., "What Do Kids Think About Computers?" *ACM SIGCUE Bulletin*, Vol. 9(3) (July 1975).

Bork, Alfred, "Learning to Teach Via Teaching the Computer to Think," *Journal of Computer-Based Instruction*, Vol 2(2) (November 1975).

Clark, Richard E., *The Best of ERIC; Recent Trends in Computer-Assisted Instruction*. Stanford, Cal.: ERIC Clearinghouse, April 1973.

Drumheller, S. J., *Handbook of Curriculum Design for Individualized Instruction: A Systems Approach*. Englewood Cliffs, N.J.: Educational Technology Publications, 1971.

Dyer, Charles, *Preparing for Computer-Assisted Instruction*. Englewood Cliffs, N.J.: Educational Technology Publications, 1972.

Everything You Always Wanted to Know about CAI But Were Afraid to Ask. Computer Uses in Education, P.O. Box 1053, Huntington Beach, Cal. 92647, 1972.

Gerry, Robert and C. Victor Bunderson, *Preparing Educational Material for Computer-Assisted Instruction*. Austin, Tex.: CAI Laboratory, The University of Texas at Austin, 1967.

Gilson, Nancy, ed., *The Author's Guide to CAI*, 3rd ed. The Ohio State University, College of Medicine, Division of Computing Services.

Hicks, B. L., and S. Hunka, *The Teacher and the Computer*. Philadelphia, Penn.: W. B. Saunders Company, 1972.

Kemp, Jerrold E., *Instructional Design*. Belmont, Cal.: Fearon Publishers, 1971.

Knief, Lotus M. and George K. Cunningham, "Effects of Tutorial CAI on Performance in Statistics," AEDS *Journal*, (Winter 1976).

Meredith, J. C., *The CAI Author Instructor*. Englewood Cliffs, N.J.: Educational Technology Publications, 1971.

Parsons, Jerry, *et al.*, "Criteria for Selecting, Evaluating or Developing Learning Modules," *Educational Technology* (February 1976).

Reed, Fay Carol, *et al.*, "A Model for the Development of Computer-Assisted Instruction Programs," *Educational Technology* (March 1974).

Simonsen, Roger H. and Kent S. Renshaw, "CAI—Boon or Boondoggle?" *Datamation* (March 1974).

Vinsonhaler, John F. and Donald K. Bass, "A Summary of Ten Major Studies on CAI Drill and Practice," *Educational Technology* (July 1972).

CHAPTER NINE

ADMINISTRATIVE COMPUTING IN MINIATURE

More than any other application (except perhaps extensive CAI with an abundance of text), administrative computing activities are severely limited by small memory size, the slowness of disk access, and the lack of special-purpose software such as data base handling routines—all inherent in the low-cost microcomputer. Common administrative applications are payroll, budget and accounting, student records, student scheduling, grade reporting, and attendance. But all these are difficult if not impossible, except on the smallest scale, using a low-cost microcomputer with under 16 k of memory and without a disk.

By "the smallest scale," we mean that while you can't handle a budget and accounting system for the whole district, you can write a program to keep track of expenses for separate, individual funds. And while it isn't feasible to do grade reporting for a 500-student school, an individual teacher can still effectively automate his or her gradebook. In the same way, a small school can keep skeletal attendance records on-line.

In most schools, the administration controls the purse strings, and sometimes the only way to get a computer purchase approved is to justify its existence by its usefulness in administrative record-keeping. For instance, programming a low-cost system to print mailing labels as a secondary activity can justify the cost of the computer for that purpose alone in a very short time. During that time, it can also provide a full program of instructional support that is worth ten times its cost in general benefit to the students. Along the same lines, even when a computer system is purchased with "instructional" funds, administrators are happier about upkeep expenditures if they have some access, even at nights and on weekends, to the system. In a typical district or school, it is sometimes politically wise to provide equal use of an expensive resource like computing.

In this chapter, we show two example programs that demonstrate the capabilities of a small, nondisk system. Each is explained in detail.

Student Information Program

The first program handles student information. The information for each student is entered in DATA statements, starting at statement number 1000. The information for each student is, in order:

Last name
First name and middle initial (or none)
Street address
Town
Zip code
Phone number
Last name of parents or guardians (in case it is different from the child's)

The user enters one of two function codes to get either the information on the student(s) with a given last name or a "mailing label" output for each student in the program. (We're not sure that mailing label paper is available for microcomputer-type printers, but if it is not now, it will be soon.) For such hard-copy output, the PRINT statements in 290 through 330 may need an added system dependent parameter to specify the printer. Here is the sample run:

```
RUN.
ENTER FUNCTION CODE (1 OR 2)
    1 = INFORMATION FOR 1 STUDENT
    2 = MAILING LABELS FOR ALL STUDENTS
?1
ENTER STUDENT'S LAST NAME
?CLARK

JAMES C. CLARK
1731 VISTA DRIVE
PLEASANTVILLE 94032
PHONE: 834-7945
PARENTS' NAME: CLARK

RALPH G. CLARK
756 STORY ROAD
KINGMAN 95401
PHONE: 542-3671
PARENTS' NAME: MALLORY
```

ENTER FUNCTION CODE (1 OR 2)

.

.

.

?2

      TO THE PARENTS OF:
          JAMES C. CLARK
          1731 VISTA DRIVE
          PLEASANTVILLE, CALIFORNIA 94032

      TO THE PARENTS OF:
          RALPH G. CLARK
          256 STORY ROAD
          KINGMAN, CALIFORNIA 95401

Description

Line(s)	Purpose
10–40	Initialization and instructions to user.
50–80	Input and check function code (FC).
90–250	Locate information for specific student(s) (function code = 1).
90–100	Input desired last name.
110–160	Read data about each student.
170–250	Test input name against just-read last name, and print all information if there's a match.
260–340	Print mailing label for each student (function code = 2).

READY.

```
10 REM STUDENT INFORMATION
20 PRINT
25 PRINT "ENTER FUNCTION CODE (1 OR 2):"
30 PRINT "   1=INFORMATION FOR 1 STUDENT"
40 PRINT "   2=MAILING LABELS FOR ALL STUDENTS"
50 INPUT FC
60 RESTORE
70 IF FC=2 GOTO 260
80 IF FC<>1 GOTO 20
90 PRINT "ENTER STUDENT'S LAST NAME"
100 INPUT IN$
110 F=0
120 READ LN$
130 IF LN$<>"ENDSTUDENTS" GOTO 160
140 IF F=0 THEN PRINT "NO SUCH NAME"
150 GOTO 20
160 READ FR$,ST$,TN$,ZP$,PH$,PN$
170 IF LN$<>IN$ GOTO 120
```

```
180 F=1
190 PRINT
200 PRINT FR$;" ";LN$
210 PRINT ST$
220 PRINT TN$;" ";ZP$
230 PRINT "PHONE: ";PH$
240 PRINT "PARENTS' NAME: ";PN$
250 GOTO 120
260 READ LN$
270 IF LN$="ENDSTUDENTS" GOTO 20
280 READ FR$,ST$,TN$,ZP$,PH$,PN$
290 PRINT
300 PRINT "TO THE PARENTS OF:"
310 PRINT "   ";FR$;" ";LN$
320 PRINT ST$
330 PRINT TN$;", CALIFORNIA ";ZP$
340 GOTO 260
1000 DATA CLARK,"JAMES C.","1731 VISTA DR.",PLEASANTVILLE,94032,
        834-7945,CLARK
1010 DATA SMITH,PATRICIA R.,1210 BIRD AVE.,REDMAN,87214,254-9542,SMITH
1020 DATA CLARK,RALPH G.,256 STORY RD.,KINGMAN,25401,542-3671,MALLORY
9998 DATA ENDSTUDENTS
9999 END
READY.
```

With such a program, additional students are added with additional DATA statements, thus requiring the program to be resaved on disk or tape. Our PET with 7 k user RAM fits about ninety students before running out of space. More RAM and/or a disk would allow more students. A more sophisticated version would keep the student information in a file on a disk; and it would use a function code (rather than a DATA statement) to add or to delete a student on the file and to update the information about a student. These three new functions, or something close to them, are always necessary in a file-based application. They form a general category of computing called *file maintenance*. Usage of files is different on each system, so you'll have to investigate.

Test Scores Program

The second program is more complicated than the first, but it still has several similar features. The purpose of the program is to "remember" test scores for up to fifteen tests for a maximum of forty students (again with DATA statements) and then to print out various statistics about the tests. The DATA statements starting at 8000 contain the student names. The test data for each test are listed at 9010, 9020, and so on) in the following order:

Test date (any format)
Weight of this test (an integer)

Scores for each student, in the same order as students are listed starting at 8000. A − 1 means no test score is available for that student. The − 1000 entries are terminators for each test and must be left alone, or more must be added if more tests are added.

The user enters one of four function codes:

1 = Print all scores for a given test, the average, and the standard deviation.
2 = Print all scores for a given student, the average, and the standard deviation.
3 = Average and standard deviation for each test.
4 = Average and standard deviation for each student.

Here is the sample run:

```
RUN
ENTER FUNCTION CODE (1, 2, 3, or 4)
    1 = SCORES FOR A GIVEN TEST
    2 = SCORES FOR GIVEN STUDENT
    3 = STATISTICS FOR ALL TESTS
    4 = STATISTICS FOR ALL STUDENTS

?1
ENTER DATE OF TEST AS DDMMMYY
?12JAN77
SCORES FOR TEST ON 12JAN77 WITH WEIGHT 1

        STUD1          50
        STUD2          10
        STUD3          10
        STUD4          75
        STUD5          10
        STUD6          10
        AVERAGE        25
        STAND DEV      26.6


ENTER FUNCTION CODE ...
?2
ENTER STUDENT'S NAME
?STUD1
```

WEIGHTS AND SCORES FOR STUD1

12JAN77	1	50
19JAN77	2	25
29JAN77	1	-1

AVERAGE 33.3   STAND DEV 14.4
ENTER FUNCTION CODE ...
?3

TEST	WEIGHT	AVERAGE	STAND DEV.
12JAN77	1	25	26.6
19JAN77	2	37.9	34.1
26JAN77	1	17	21.7

AVERAGE OF THE AVERAGE SCORES 29.4
STAND DEV. OF THE AVERAGE SCORES 10.3
ENTER FUNCTION CODE ...
?4

NAME	AVERAGE	STAND DEV
STUD1	33.3	14.4
STUD2	52.5	55
STUD3	41.3	21
STUD4	65	8.7
STUD5	10	0
STUD6	10	0
STUD7	10	0

AVERAGE OF THE AVERAGE SCORES 31.7
STAND DEV OF AVERAGE SCORES   22.5

ENTER FUNCTION CODE ...

Program description

Variable	Usage
N$(I)	Students' names.
D$(I)	Test dates
W%(I)	Weights for each test, in integer format (specified by "%") to save space.
S%(I,J)	Test scores for each test ("I" dimension) and each student ("J" dimension), in integer format.
NP	Number of pupils.
NT	Number of tests.

FC	Function code.
TS	Sum of (weighted) test averages.
TQ	(Weighted) sum of the square of the averages.
TN	Number of weights or tests.
SUM	(Weighted) sum of the scores.
SSQ	(Weighted) sum of the squares of the test scores.
NS	(Weighted) sum of the number of tests.

Line(s)	Purpose
10–110	Initialization.
15	"3" represents the CLEAR SCREEN code for a PET.
60	− 1 indicates no test score.
120–390	Read DATA statements and save in arrays.
400–410	Get function code.
420	Clears the screen.
430–450	Determines proper routine to execute based on the value of function code.
460–580	Processing for function code = 1.
550	If there are fewer than two tests, there is no average or standard deviation.
590–680	Processing for function code = 2.
690–910	Processing for function code = 3.
760	If no tests, there is no average or standard deviation.
830	If only one test, cannot compute standard deviation.
920–1110	Processing for function code = 4.
1120–1220	Go through all scores for all students ("J" variable) for a given test ("I" variable).
1160	If function code is 1, print individual names and test scores.
1230–1330	Go through all scores for all tests ("I" variable) for a given student ("J" variable).
1270	If function code is 2, print individual dates, weights, and test scores.

```
READY.
10 DIM N$(41),D$(15),W%(15),S%(15,40)
15 PRINT "3INITIALIZING"
20 FOR I=1 TO 15
30 D$(I)=""
40 W%(I)=0
50 FOR J=1 TO 40
60 S%(I,J)=-1
70 NEXT J
80 NEXT I
90 FOR I=1 TO 40
100 N$(I)=""
110 NEXT I
120 PRINT"READING DATA BASE"
130 RESTORE
```

```
140 FOR I=1 TO 41
150 READ N$(I)
160 IF N$(I)="ENDNAMES" GOTO 200
170 NEXT I
180 PRINT"TOO MANY STUDENTS"
190 END
200 NP=I-1
210 FOR I=1 TO 15
220 READ D$(I)
230 IF D$(I)="ENDTESTS" GOTO 390
240 J=0
250 READ W%(I)
260 IF W%(I)=-1000 GOTO 360
270 FOR J=1 TO 40
280 READ S%(I,J)
290 IF S%(I,J)=-1000 GOTO 360
300 NEXT J
320 READ L
330 IF L=-1000 GOTO 360
340 PRINT"TOO MANY TEST SCORES ON ";D$(I)
350 END
360 IF NP<>J-1 THEN PRINT NP;" STUDENTS AND";J-1;" SCORES ON ";D$(I)
370 NEXT I
390 NT=I-1
400 PRINT
401 PRINT"ENTER FUNCTION CODE (1,2,3, OR 4)"
402 PRINT " 1=SCORES FOR GIVEN TEST"
403 PRINT " 2=SCORES FOR GIVEN STUDENT"
404 PRINT " 3=STATISTICS FOR ALL TESTS"
405 PRINT " 4=STATISTICS FOR ALL STUDENTS"
410 INPUT FC
420 PRINT"3"
430 ON FC GOTO 460,590,690,920
440 PRINT"INVALID CODE"
450 GOTO 400
460 PRINT"ENTER DATE OF TEST AS DDMMMYY"
470 INPUT A$
480 FOR I=1 TO NT
490 IF D$(I)=A$ GOTO 530
500 NEXT I
510 PRINT"NO SUCH DATE"
520 GOTO 400
530 PRINT"SCORES FOR TEST ON ";A$;" WITH WEIGHT";W%(I)
540 GOSUB 1120
550 IF NS<2 GOTO 400
560 PRINT"AVERAGE",INT(SUM/NS*10+.5)/10
570 PRINT"STAND DEV",INT(SQR((SSQ-SUM*SUM/NS)/(NS-1))*10+.5)/10
580 GOTO 400
590 PRINT"ENTER STUDENT'S NAME"
600 INPUT A$
610 FOR J=1 TO NP
620 IF N$(J)=A$ GOTO 660
630 NEXT J
640 PRINT"NO SUCH NAME"
650 GOTO 400
660 PRINT"WEIGHTS AND SCORES FOR ";A$
670 GOSUB 1230
680 GOTO 550
690 PRINT " TEST    WEIGHT      AVERAGE    STAND DEV"
695 PRINT
700 TS=0
710 TQ=0
720 TN=0
730 FOR I=1 TO NT
740 GOSUB 1120
750 PRINT D$(I),W%(I);
760 IF NS>0 GOTO 790
770 PRINT ,"NA","NA"
780 GOTO 870
790 AV=SUM/NS
800 TS=TS+AV*W%(I)
810 TQ=TQ+AV*AV*W%(I)
820 TN=TN+W%(I)
```

```
830 IF NS>1 GOTO 860
840 PRINT ,INT(AV*10+.5)/10,"NA"
850 GOTO 870
860 PRINT ,INT(AV*10+.5)/10,INT(SQR((SSQ-SUM*SUM/NS)/(NS-1))*10+.5)/10
870 NEXT I
880 IF TN<2 GOTO 400
890 PRINT"AVERAGE OF THE AVERAGE SCORES",INT(TS/TN*10+.5)/10
900 PRINT"STAND DEV OF AVERAGE SCORES",INT(SQR((TQ-TS*TS/TN)/(TN-1))*10+.5)/10
910 GOTO 400
920 PRINT " NAME     AVERAGE   STAND DEV"
925 PRINT
930 TS=0
940 TQ=0
950 TN=0
960 FOR J=1 TO NP
970 GOSUB 1230
990 IF NS>0 GOTO 1020
1000 PRINT N$(J),"NA","NA"
1010 GOTO 1100
1020 AV=SUM/NS
1030 TS=TS+AV
1040 TQ=TQ+AV*AV
1050 TN=TN+1
1060 IF NS>1 GOTO 1090
1070 PRINT N$(J),INT(AV*10+.5)/10,"NA"
1080 GOTO 1100
1090 PRINT N$(J),INT(AV*10+.5)/10,INT(SQR((SSQ-SUM*SUM/NS)/(NS-1))*10+.5)/10
1100 NEXT J
1110 GOTO 880
1120 SUM=0
1130 SSQ=0
1140 NS=0
1150 FOR J=1 TO NP
1160 IF FC=1 THEN PRINT N$(J),S%(I,J)
1170 IF S%(I,J)=-1 GOTO 1210
1180 SUM=SUM+S%(I,J)
1190 SSQ=SSQ+S%(I,J)*S%(I,J)
1200 NS=NS+1
1210 NEXT J
1220 RETURN
1230 SUM=0
1240 SSQ=0
1250 NS=0
1260 FOR I=1 TO NT
1270 IF FC=2 THEN PRINT D$(I),W%(I),S%(I,J)
1280 IF S%(I,J)=-1 GOTO 1320
1290 SUM=SUM+S%(I,J)*W%(I)
1300 SSQ=SSQ+S%(I,J)*S%(I,J)*W%(I)
1310 NS=NS+W%(I)
1320 NEXT I
1330 RETURN
8000 DATA STUD1,STUD2,STUD3,STUD4
8001 DATA STUDENT5,STUDENT6,STUDENT7
8999 DATA ENDNAMES
9010 DATA 12JAN77,1,50,10,10,75
9011 DATA 10,10,10
9019 DATA -1000
9020 DATA 19JAN77,2,25,100,50,60
9021 DATA 10,10,10
9029 DATA -1000
9030 DATA 26JAN77,1,-1,0,55,-1
9031 DATA 10,10,10
9039 DATA -1000
9998 DATA ENDTESTS
9999 END
READY.
```

Although this program was developed on a PET, it will not currently work on a PET, except for very small examples as shown in this program. This shortcoming is due to a bug in the BASIC that calculates array locations modulo 256 (thus overlaying array locations 1–256 with the contents of array elements above 256). Since the BASIC is in ROM, we cannot fix this bug; and Commodore is currently being unresponsive to those of us struggling with earlier models. The defect has, however, been fixed for current production runs, so a new PET should be all right. It is easy to test with the following program:

```
10  DIM A (300)
20  A (1) = 1
30  A (257) = 257
40  PRINT A (1)
```

If the program prints 1, the bug has been fixed. If it prints 257, the bug is still there.

Like the first program, this program can be enhanced by keeping the data in a file on a disk. Again, new software for file maintenance is necessary to:

1. add students,
2. delete students,
3. add tests, or
4. modify test scores, especially in changing a −1 (no score) after a make-up test is given

All four of these functions can be done in the example program by direct manipulation of the DATA statements. But such direct manipulation is not possible once the data is placed in a file.

A variation of the test scores program can be written to keep attendance. The first set of data statements consists again of a list of all student names. Each subsequent DATA statement contains the date and a list of the absent students for that date. Function codes would be similar:

1 = Print all absentees for a given date and the total number.
2 = Print all absent days for a given student and the total number.
3 = Total number of absentees for each date.
4 = Total number of absent days for each student.

Since the number of absentees would presumably be small for any one day, the data might be read not into arrays for processing but rather directly from the DATA statements, as many times as necessary.

Such an attendance program would probably not be as useful as the test scores program on a nondisk system, since it must be used every day (read, updated with a new DATA statement, and rewritten) and since it performs no time-consuming function like calculating averages and standard deviations. But it is still interesting to note the similarity in the structures of the programs for two seemingly dissimilar applications.

Summary

As the cost/performance ratio for microcomputer hardware continues to decrease, more extensive record-keeping will become feasible with computer systems that carry rock-bottom price tags. Low-cost disk drives and software, to build and to maintain large banks of administrative data, are currently the only barriers to full scale administrative computing on a very modest machine. It is only a matter of time before these barriers, too, are struck down.

CHAPTER TEN

WHERE TO GO FOR HELP

The possibilities of computer applications to education can be mind-boggling to the person just introduced to them. Chapters 1–9 described only the applications that can reasonably be attempted with a microcomputer limited in memory size and speed. Though enough examples have been given to allow experimentation in a variety of subjects, enthusiastic teachers quickly exhaust these examples and become hungry for more—more programs, more proven curriculum materials, and more subject-specific theory and evaluation results.

These teachers can rest assured that plenty of help is available to them. A wealth of student materials exists in BASIC; the challenge is to access it and effectively to sort that which is useful from that which is not. In this chapter, we list sources for some of these materials as well as sources for help in sorting them. Sometimes these sources are one and the same.

Special Interest Groups and Publications

Professional Organizations/Conferences

At least five professional organizations are firmly committed to computer use in education. Three are concerned exclusively with computers in education, while the other two are associations of teachers of two particular subjects that are especially amenable to computer application.

1. The *National Council of Teachers of Mathematics (NCTM)* has been heavily involved with computer-assisted mathematics for more than a decade. Many sessions at the annual NCTM meeting are devoted to computer mathematics and techniques for teaching it. Workshops and tutorials of a how-to-do-it nature are presented, and a number of highly knowledgeable people are always in attendance at the conference. NCTM headquarters offers a list of

publications that includes several excellent computer and calculator-related works, and the organization also publishes the highly regarded periodical, *The Mathematics Teacher*, which treats computer topics quite regularly. For more information and a list of publications, you can write to:

NCTM
1906 Association Drive
Reston, Virginia 22091

2. The *National Science Teachers Association (NSTA)* has been equally as interested in computer-based science instruction. This interest is reflected in the presentations at each year's NSTA conference. *The Science Teacher*, published by NSTA, periodically publishes articles about computer applications in biology, chemistry, physics, and general science. For information, write:

National Science Teachers Association
1742 Connecticut Avenue, N.W.
Washington, D.C. 20009

3. The largest educational computing organization is the *Association for Educational Data Systems (AEDS)*, which is composed of nearly equal representations from administrative and instructional computer users; the group is mostly secondary level people. AEDS holds an annual conference, publishes a Proceedings from each conference, sponsors regional workshops in special interest areas, and publishes the *AEDS Monitor*, a magazine presenting articles on educational data processing. All these activities split their focuses between administration and instruction. You can join AEDS or send for the Proceedings from recent conferences by writing:

Association for Educational Data Systems
1201 Sixteenth Street, N.W.
Washington, D.C. 20036

4. The *Conference on Computers in the Undergraduate Curricula (CCUC)* is an annual conference, sponsored in part by the National Science Foundation and devoted to the instructional use of computers in colleges and universities. Proceedings for past conferences (1970–1978) are available for $10 each from:

CCUC
Lindquist Center for Measurement
University of Iowa
Iowa City, Iowa 52242

5. The *Association for the Development of Computer-Based Instructional Systems (ADCIS)* is primarily concerned with computer-assisted instruction designed for use in the health sciences curriculum. ADCIS holds a yearly meeting and publishes a quarterly journal, *Journal of Computer-Based Instruction.* For membership and/or subscription information, write:

> Joan Lauer Hayes
> ADCIS Secretary/Treasurer
> Computer Center
> Western Washington State College
> Bellingham, Washington 98225

Involvement with one or more of these organizations is richly rewarding. The conferences are valuable not only because of the formal presentations but also because of the informal sharing of ideas and experiences that quite naturally occurs. Contacting other people with similar interests and goals is the most important research activity you can undertake. These people can and will provide valuable insights and aid when you find yourself in a dilemma or at what seems to be a dead end.

Relevant Periodicals

The number of magazines and journals concerned with educational computing, computer games, and/or microcomputers and home computers is truly staggering. A list of some of these periodicals follows, with a brief description of each and subscription information. The first group of magazines is educational in nature, with content of direct interest to the educator:

1. *Creative Computing* has been described as the *Scientific American* of the personal computing field. It is an educational/recreational magazine that appeals to computer users of all kinds. *Creative Computing* presents articles on particular applications, programming techniques, comparisons of high-level languages, the applications for which certain of these languages are most appropriate, collections of problems that are solvable by computer and others that are not, discussions of the sociological impact of computers, complete listings of games and puzzles, and an excellent book review section. In short, *Creative Computing* is an outstanding publication, and we consider it a *must* for anyone involved with or interested in educational or home computing. *Creative Computing* is published bi-monthly, and is available for $8 per year* from:

*All subscription rates quoted in this chapter are for U.S. subscriptions only.

Creative Computing
P.O. Box 789–M
Morristown, New Jersey 07960

2. *People's Computers*, the new name for the *PCC Newspaper*, is a
magazine aimed at the education/recreation market. Its content,
mostly descriptive articles on classroom applications and games
with detailed examples, is suitable for the beginning through intermediate computer user. *People's Computers* is available for $8 a
year from:

PCC
P.O. Box E
Menlo Park, California 94025

3. *Dr. Dobb's Journal of Computer Calisthenics and Orthodontia*,
also published by the People's Computer Company, is described as
a reference journal for users of home computers. It was begun as a
means for conveying public domain software such as the Tiny
BASIC language. Complete source code listings for such software
are often included, along with consumer notes on computer
products and fairly technical discussions of hardware and software.
More a newsletter than a magazine, *Dr. Dobb's* contains articles
and other tidbits of interest to the sophisticated user concerned with
state-of-the-art details. Published ten times a year and obtainable
for $12 per year or $1.50 per single issue, you can get *Dr. Dobb's
Journal* from:

Dr. Dobb's Journal
P.O. Box E
Menlo Park, California 94025

4. *Calculators/Computers*, edited by Don Inman and published by
Dymax, was developed to supply practical computing material for
educational purposes. Like *People's Computers*, its content is
suitable for beginning through intermediate computer users, but it
contains more practical, how-to information. Special emphasis is
placed on ready-to-use classroom units, and permission is given to
copy these materials for noncommercial purposes. Content is split
roughly half and half between calculators and computers.
Problems, games, and general hints for using calculators and
computers are also included in the magazine. Subscription rates are
$12 per year. Write:

Dymax
P.O. Box 310
Menlo Park, California 94025

5. *Educational Technology*, published monthly, contains articles on the application of all types of educational technology, but computers are heavily represented in the articles presented over the last seven or eight years. Articles are usually theoretical but interesting and informative, often providing supporting data for preferences developed among experienced educational computer users. Articles cover the range of educational computer applications. We highly recommend this magazine for the educator who wants to know *why*. *Educational Technology* is available for $25 per year from:

> Educational Technology Publications
> 140 Sylvan Avenue
> Englewood Cliffs, New Jersey 07632

6. *Journal of Educational Technology Systems*, published quarterly, is a very technical educational journal whose articles typically discuss the mathematical models underlying curriculum or program development. Recommended for developers of curriculum projects or instructional support systems, this journal is available for $33 per year from:

> Baywood Publishing Company
> 43 Central Drive
> Farmingdale, New York 11735

7. *Popular Computing*, edited and published by Fred Gruenberger, regularly contains a collection of complex, intriguing programming problems. Programs are included that are a challenge for each level of programmer from secondary computer science student to experienced software designers. This extended-newsletter publication can be ordered for $15 per year (prepaid order only) from:

> Popular Computing
> P.O. Box 272
> Calabasas, California 91302

8. *SIGCUE Bulletin*, published quarterly by the Special Interest Group on Computer Use in Education of the Association for Computing Machinery (ACM), presents excellent interviews with some of the leaders in educational computing, coverage of nationwide conferences, updates on current projects, articles on specific applications and/or application types, and a good reference list from current publications. It is available for $5 per year to ACM members, $12.50 to nonmembers, and $16.50 to institutions. Write:

> Association for Computing Machinery
> 1133 Avenue of the Americas
> New York, New York 10036

9. *Simulation/Gaming*, published five times a year by a group at the University of Idaho (with contributing authors from all over the country), is an excellent source of information on game design, new games that have been developed, and the effective use of games in the classroom. Occasionally, articles are printed on computer games, but usually this is not the case. It is available for $6 per year from:

Simulation/Gaming
P.O. Box 3039, University Station
Moscow, Idaho 83843

The other group of periodicals is oriented toward microcomputers and home computing:

1. *BYTE* magazine, published monthly, contains detailed hardware and software discussions on small computers and micro-peripherals. The information offered is on a very technical level but useful for the person constructing a home-brewed system or programming in a machine-language environment. It is available for $12 per year from:

BYTE Subscriptions
P.O. Box 361
Arlington, Massachusetts 02174

2. *Kilobaud*, also a monthly magazine, is a how-to-do-it publication for both hardware and software enthusiasts. The level of sophistication of the articles covers a wide range. Available for $15 per year from:

Kilobaud
Peterborough, New Hampshire 03458

Users Groups—Past and Present

If a users group has been organized for your computer, this is an exceptional resource for ready-to-run programs since they will run without modification on your machine (as long as the configuration is the same). A users group is also an excellent way to make contact with other educators with similar interests and goals. Users groups for other machines are also potentially useful as a source of information—especially if their machine uses the same type and level of BASIC as yours.

Even users groups for minicomputer vendors can be useful to you, since they sometimes have either special interest groups for education, an educational program library, or a list of available curriculum materials. Although programs designed for minicomputers might need some modification, in many cases they are still preferable to starting from scratch.

One users group that we are intimately acquainted with is the Hewlett-Packard Educational Users Group. HP's group holds regional and national meetings in conjunction with key educational conferences, and it has published an excellent newsletter since 1972. Applications stories, games, programs, book reviews, and articles on the why and how of educational computing are regularly included. Past issues are available for a nominal price from:

> HP Educational Users Group
> General Systems Division
> 19400 Homestead Road
> Cupertino, California 95014

Bibliographies Available

Over the years, a number of bibliographies have been compiled by people working with computers in education. Some of these bibliographies are general-purpose, and some are oriented toward specific topics. Those we know of are listed below:

> Kiewit Computation Center
> Dartmouth College
> Hanover, New Hampshire 03755

Kiewit offers a list of general- and special-purpose publications developed under Project COMPUTe because of Dartmouth's early and continued commitment to free-access computing for all students. Some excellent materials are included on this list.

> Center for Research in Learning and Teaching (CRLT)
> University of Michigan
> 109 East Madison Street
> Ann Arbor, Michigan 48104

Two documents are available from CRLT: "Free and Inexpensive Materials in Teaching and Learning—An Informal Appraisal" and "Suggested Sources: A Reference Shelf for Educators Considering Use of Computers in the Instructional Process."

> CERL
> University of Illinois
> Urbana, Illinois 61801

CERL offers a list of documents available pertaining to the PLATO IV Project.

CONDUIT
University of Iowa
Iowa City, Iowa 52242

College level curriculum materials are available through CONDUIT that have been evaluated for transportability. Write for information on how to join CONDUIT.

P.O. Box E
School of Education
Stanford University
Stanford, California 94305

A document entitled "Recent Trends in Computer-Assisted Instruction" is available, containing abstracts of some 39 reports, articles, and books.

Computing Newsletter
University of Colorado
Colorado Springs, Colorado 80907

Computing Newsletter compiles an annual bibliography of computer-oriented books for $4. Over 1,200 books are categorized by subject area.

Clearinghouses

ERIC (Educational Resources Information Center) is a nationwide information network for acquiring, selecting, abstracting, indexing, storing, retrieving, and disseminating the most significant and timely educational research reports and projects. ERIC consists of a coordinating staff in Washington, D.C., and 19 clearinghouses across the country, each of which is responsible for a particular educational area. For information, write:

ERIC
U.S. Office of Education
400 Maryland Avenue, S.W.
Washington, D.C. 20202

SIE (Smithsonian Science Information Exchange) is a clearinghouse service for research in progress under federal contracts and grants. Abstracts are available, accessed by computer search on keywords.

HP Clearinghouse for Computer Applications to Education catalogs more than 300 items in four categories: (1) instructional applications, (2) administrative applications (cataloged by application type),

(3) educational utility packages (diagnostics, language modifications, and the like), and (4) references. The entries are cross-referenced through the use of special-purpose indexes. Information for each entry includes a description, computer requirements, and source information. The HP Clearinghouse Catalog is available for $4 from the HP Educational Users Group address noted in the "Users Group" section; the order number is 5955-1703.

Statewide Organizations

Some states have a statewide time-sharing network or a regulatory committee involved with computer education. Such groups can be a valuable resource. Often they offer program libraries, teacher training courses, and curriculum evaluation and/or development. Some such groups are TIES and MECC in Minnesota, the RCC in Iowa, and OTIS in Oregon, but there are others. If you are already associated with such a group and adding one or more microcomputers to augment your time-sharing program, the group can still be of help, albeit in an indirect and limited manner. You can probably receive permission to use the program library, but modifications to make the programs run on your computer are your responsibility. The other services are usually as applicable for stand-alone microcomputer use as for time-sharing port/terminal use.

A Final Routing to Chapter References

At the end of each chapter in this book, we have included a comprehensive list of references pertaining to the topic discussed. These references are invaluable to educators interested in further pursuing these specific topics; not only are the references worthwhile for researching ideas and experiences, but they too contain references, that contain references, that contain references, and so on. As we said at the beginning of this chapter, there is plenty of help for the teacher who is sincerely interested in promoting his or her knowledge and experience of computer applications to education. The problem lies in zeroing in on your interest area.

CHAPTER ELEVEN

DECIDING WHAT TO BUY

Microcomputer systems in 1978 run the gamut from primitive put-together machine-language-only systems to complete computer systems with up to 192k-bytes of memory and such peripherals as dual floppy disk drives, line printers, CRT and graphics terminals, and special-purpose devices such as voice and music synthesizers. Correspondingly, the prices cover the whole spectrum too, from under $500 to around $10,000 for the most elaborate system in this class. Consequently, deciding on *the* best system is an exceedingly difficult task.

The first step in choosing a computer system is to carefully analyze your needs, determine your goals, and assess your resources. This initial step should narrow your choices considerably. As the next step, read the rest of this chapter, which discusses the levels of software and the machines that support them. Finally, once the field has been narrowed to just a few systems, spend some time trying out each of the choices, familiarize yourself with its special features, and decide just how useful these (often costly) features are in your environment. Then buy the system that provides the most computing power for the money, relative to your needs.

Discussion of the Classic Debates

Which Processor for You?

Quite frankly, you probably don't care. The main reason you might care is if you plan to program in machine or assembly language. But, in that case, you must be experienced enough to have your own biases about processors and instruction architecture, and you can therefore make your own decisions based on those biases.

The other reason you might be concerned about the processor is its speed. It is true that some processors are faster than others. However, such differences can easily be overshadowed by the way BASIC is implemented, such that a nominally faster CPU might execute its BASIC more slowly than a nominally slower CPU. If you are worried about speed, select a category of machines to support your needs from the discussions that follow. Then write one or more programs (called "benchmarks") of the type you will use on your system, and run each program on each processor in that category to determine the true overall speed.

BASIC in RAM or ROM?

A relatively recent innovation is the ability to store the BASIC interpreter (which itself is a program) in ROM. If BASIC is to execute in RAM, it must be loaded into RAM from some I/O device. But if BASIC is to execute in ROM, it comes already in ROM from the factory and never needs to be loaded. The advantage of ROM BASIC lies mainly in its use on small systems whose I/O devices would require a long time to load BASIC into RAM. BASIC in a ROM is instantly available after powering up, with no need to load it into memory. And, since a program in ROM cannot be altered, BASIC cannot be "wiped out" (and thus require reloading) by a programming bug.

However, this nonalterability also gives rise to the disadvantage of ROM BASIC—bugs in the BASIC interpreter itself cannot easily be changed as they can if BASIC is in RAM. Thus you are at the mercy of the manufacturer to make replacement ROMs available at a reasonable price in a reasonable length of time.

On balance, we recommend BASIC in ROM for minimum configurations with only slow I/O devices (the front panel, paper tape, cassette tape, and the like). For systems with a disk, you still need at least a disk bootstrap in ROM (to get programs from the disk into RAM), but it is not very important for BASIC to be in ROM since the loading time from disk is so short. Thus, in a disk system, we recommend BASIC in RAM so that it can be debugged, extended, and modified in other ways.

How Much Memory?

ROM is no problem—you take the amount the manufacturer uses in the system, since less won't work and more you can't use. How much RAM to buy depends on two factors:

1. Is BASIC in ROM or RAM?
2. What applications do you plan?

Your real interest is the amount of RAM you have available for programs and data, which we will call *user RAM*. Thus, if BASIC is in RAM, you need more RAM than if BASIC is in ROM. For instance, if you need 8k of user RAM for your applications and BASIC uses 4k of RAM, then you need 12k. But be careful and ask good questions: Manufacturers tend to be less than truthful about the size of their BASICs, and you might find you've bought an "8k BASIC" that takes 11k! Also, even though BASIC might be in ROM, it will use some amount of RAM for working storage since intermediate results cannot be stored in ROM. For instance, our PET uses about 1,024 bytes of RAM for working storage. However, remember that the memories on almost all systems are expandable to at least 32k—all it takes is money. As a guideline, consider the following:

1. All the programs in this book, other than the simulations in Chapter 6 and the administrative applications in Chapter 9, will run in 4k of user RAM. This includes computer science (Chapter 4), problem-solving (Chapter 5), games (Chapter 7), and CAI (Chapter 8). Exceptions to each are possible:
   a. An advanced computer science class might require 8k-16k—or more—of user RAM.
   b. Complex problems can require more RAM.
   c. Some very fancy games (like the Star Trek variety) require more RAM.
   d. A sophisticated CAI program that remembers the results of each student, selects the level of study for each student based on past results, and performs other evaluative tasks would require 8k-32k of user RAM.
2. Simulations of the sort shown in this book take 8k of user RAM. Of course, more sophisticated simulations require even more RAM.
3. The administrative uses demonstrated in this book were squeezed uncomfortably into 8k (actually 7k, since 1k is lost to working storage). You'd better count on 16k for limited applications and 32k or more for extensive applications.
4. Time-sharing is a real memory hog—better count on 32k and up.

Tape or Disk Storage?

You certainly need one and maybe both. Tape storage is cheaper but slower. If your needs are such that you will load one program, run it for several hours (without using files), and then go on to another program, then you probably don't need a disk. But if you will be changing programs often or using data files, you probably need a disk. In an educational environment, you will probably *need* a disk only if you plan on administrative applications, but disks are almost always desirable.

CRT or Hard-Copy Terminal?

Again, you certainly need one and maybe both. A small CRT is cheaper than a hard-copy device, even though it allows faster and fancier output, especially when playing games on the computer. However, without a hard-copy device, no outputs can be saved, short of photographing the screen. If you plan to use only programs prepared by others and supplied to you on tape or disk, and if these programs perform properly in a CRT-only environment, then you can probably survive with only a CRT. However, if you plan to make your own programs and/or use hard-copy-oriented programs (such as those that produce plots, tables of answers, mailing labels, etc.), you'd better count on a hard-copy device. Whether this output replaces the CRT or supplements it depends on your needs. For educational uses, the superiority of the CRT in interactive use leads us to recommend that the CRT be kept even if a hard-copy device is added.

Today's Products

In an educational environment, the quality of the high-level language determines the usefulness of the computer system; the type of processor or other hardware details is not particularly important. The primary consideration in choosing a computer for educational use, then, should be the level of BASIC that is supported, coupled with special considerations concerning the breadth of the program planned. The following discussion of systems and their salient features centers primarily on the BASIC language offered with each. Available peripherals and even ease of use are considered secondary, though still important, considerations. At the end of the discussion is a table of popular microcomputer models with feature comparisons and price information.

Category One—Machine-Language-Only Computers

The lowest-cost computers consist of a processor, a small amount of memory, a power supply, optional interfaces, and a front panel. They are programmable in machine language only, and often they don't include an input/output device other than the switches and display on the front panel. Note that a machine-language-only system doesn't have to be small or inexpensive, and in fact it can be a very powerful system; regardless, it is not well suited to most educational applications, and so we have left it out of our discussion. In an advanced computer science class, a machine language system can be a valuable learning tool; but in beginning classes and other instructional situations, its complexity is a hindrance rather than a help.

Category Two—"Tiny"BASIC

The next category of computer systems generally offers more memory and includes a rather primitive BASIC interpreter. Tiny BASIC is a functional subset of standard BASIC, uses between 2 and 3k of memory, and includes the fundamental statements and commands. However, string handling, arrays, and floating point arithmetic are notably lacking, along with many of the special functions.

Some manufacturers offer a more extensive but still limited version of BASIC that provides single dimension array capabilities and floating point arithmetic—thus bridging the wide applications gap between Tiny BASIC and the typical 8k BASIC that is described in Category Three.

While educational applications can be programmed in Tiny BASIC, floating point is needed for realistic problem-solving, and multiple-dimensioned arrays are needed for many simulation and game applications.

One of the standard Tiny BASICs, offered by Itty Bitty Computer Co., is described as follows:

Commands
CLEAR　　　RUN　　　LIST

Statements
PRINT　　　GOTO　　　REM
INPUT　　　GOSUB　　END
LET　　　　RETURN　　IF...THEN

Operators
Arithmetic operators only (integer arithmetic only)

Variables
26 variables only (A-Z). Variable range: —32,768 to + 32,767
No string variables

Functions
RND and USR only

The limitations of Tiny BASIC are more apparent when you look at the description of 8k BASIC in the next category.

Computer systems supporting Tiny BASIC or extended Tiny BASIC are, briefly, as follows:

Apple II

Apple Computer, Inc.
10260 Bandley Drive
Cupertino, California 95014

The Apple II is one of the most attractive game playing computers on the market today. Its most unique feature is its ability to support graphics in fifteen different colors, providing remarkable versatility for game set-ups. Two game paddle controllers are also included.

Apple BASIC is more sophisticated than standard Tiny BASIC because of the graphics commands, game paddle read function, string variables, and SGN, ASC, and LEN functions. A line number trace and variable trace can be initiated, and I/O device assignments can be switched. It is limited to integer arithmetic only and has no disk option.

Apple prices are quite high for the minimal configuration because of the extensive graphics, but the add-on memory needed to make use of that capability is very reasonable.

Tandy TRS-80 (Radio Shack). The Tandy TRS-80 consists of four modules: (1) the keyboard, (2) the video monitor, (3) the computer, and (4) cassette recorder, plus a power pack for the computer. It comes with 4k of ROM (containing Level I BASIC) and 4k of RAM; an external connector is provided at the back of the keyboard unit to add up to 32k of memory.

Level I BASIC is slightly more powerful than the typical Tiny BASIC: FOR...NEXT loops are allowed, three additional functions (ABS, INT, and TAB) are available, and relational operators $<$, $>$, $=$, $<>$, $<=$, $>=$ are allowed. A very sketchy graphics capability is also included.

There are only three error codes offered: WHAT (unintelligible instruction), HOW (instruction cannot be executed), and SORRY (you have run out of memory). As partial compensation for this, however, you can instruct the machine to indicate the exact position of the error in a faulty statement, and a question mark appears at the point where the error occurs.

Two string variables, each limited to sixteen characters, are allowed, and a single array can also be employed. The RND function will return pseudo-random numbers between 0 and 1, or between 1 and a specified number X [RND (16) returns numbers between 1 and 16]. Editing is very limited, in that a line with an error must be completely retyped to correct it. On the other hand, the LIST command incorporates a very handy feature—only sixteen lines are displayed at once—typing an up arrow scrolls up the next 16 lines, and so forth.

SOL Systems I and II

Processor Technology
6200 Hollis Street
Emeryville, California 94608

The SOL System I consists of a SOL-20 with 8k of RAM, a video monitor, cassette recorder, and a tape of the 5k BASIC available for this system. One of the most powerful Tiny BASICs, the 5k BASIC adds XEQ (get and run), CALL (to call a machine-language subroutine), DIM, FOR...NEXT, file handling, and a variety of functions (ABS, ARG, COS, INT, SGN, SIN, SQR, STR, TAB, and TAN in addition to RND). Neither string handling nor floating point arithmetic is available.

The System II is essentially the same system but with 16k of RAM, enabling the user to write much longer programs. The price differential between the 8k and 16k systems is very little, making the System II particularly attractive.

Both the System I and System II are available either in kit form or assembled and tested.

The Digital Group System I
The Digital Group
P.O. Box 6528
Denver, Colorado 80206

The philosophy of the Digital Group is to design systems that can easily be adapted to take advantage of advances in technology. They are particularly sensitive to the short life of the processor. All system components are independent of the CPU, and in fact systems are available based on the Z-80, 8080, 6800, and MOS Technology 6501/6502.

System I is based on a Z-80 with 10k of RAM and has the interfaces for a video monitor and audio cassette recorder/player. Two versions of (extended) Tiny BASIC are offered: one adds string handling, and the other adds single dimensioned variables.

SWTPC 6800
Southwest Technical Products
219 W. Rhapsody
San Antonio, Texas 78216

Sold in kit form only, the SWTPC 6800 includes 4k of ROM and 4k of RAM. Memory is expandable to 32k. Also available is 4k BASIC that includes the commands and statements typical for a small BASIC, with a few added statements such as ON...GOTO, ON...GOSUB, and PATCH. Five functions besides RND and USR are offered, and relational operators are allowed. The 4k BASIC requires 6k and preferably 8k of RAM.

Category Three—8k BASIC

A machine that supports a typical 8k version of BASIC (most of which were written by a company called Microsoft) is the minimum configuration recommended for the range of applications presented in this book. Such a machine can accept programs from most microcomputers and many minicomputers: Commodore PET, OSI Challenger II and III, SWTP 6800/2, Altair 8080, Altair 680, IMSAI 8080, Processor Technology SOL-20, PDP-8, and PDP-11 to name a few. The main advantage of using a machine that supports this BASIC is that there is an almost endless source for application programs and games. Programs written in BASIC for these machines are virtually interchangeable, though an occasional statement differs in format from one to another, necessitating minor modifications to the source program.

Comparing 8k BASIC to the Tiny BASIC described earlier, it is obvious that more diversified programming is possible. Floating point arithmetic and string manipulation greatly increase the complexity of the applications that can be implemented. The following features are only those that are *added* to Tiny BASIC:

Commands
CONT   NEW

Statements
PEEK   POKE   FOR. . .NEXT   READ   RESTORE
IF...GOTO   DATA   DIM   DEF

Operators
Logical operators (NOT, AND, OR)
Relational operators ($<$, $>$, $<$ $>$, $<$ =, $>$ =, =)

Functions
Trigonometric functions (ATN, COS, SIN, TAN, ATN)
Logarithmic functions (LOG, EXP)
Formatting functions (POS, EXP)
FRE (tells you how much memory space is still available)
INT (returns the integer portion of a floating point number)
SGN (returns a code to indicate the sign of a number)
ABS (returns absolute value)
SQR (returns square root)

String Functions
ASC (ASCII Value) RIGHT (right-hand portion of string)
LEFT (left-hand portion of string) MID (mid-section of string)
CHR (decimal value of character) STR (convert number to string)
LEN (string length) VAL (convert string to number)

There are many computer systems that offer some form of 8k BASIC. Extended versions offer such extra features as formatted output, statement renumbering, multi-line user-defined functions, point plotting on the video display, or string concatenation. The most popular 8k systems are:

Commodore PET

Commodore Business Machines
901 California Avenue
Palo Alto, California 94303

The Commodore PET has been thoroughly described in Chapters 3 and 4. It is the only completely encased system currently available, with computer, keyboard, CRT, and cassette recorder/player all in one package. PET BASIC, a full implementation of 8k BASIC, is provided in ROM; and 4k and 8k RAM models of the PET are available. Memory expansion up to 32k is possible, but anything above 8k is external to the case. A printer is available, and a floppy disk is planned for the future. Our only reservation regarding the PET is its small keyboard, with the keys undersized and close together, making touch typing difficult if not impossible. Nevertheless, we feel that the PET is a very capable system, well suited to educational use, and a good buy at the price.

Challenger IIP

Ohio Scientific
11681 Hayden Street
Hiram, Ohio 44234

The Challenger IIP includes 8k of ROM, 4k of RAM, an audio cassette interface, and a keyboard; a video monitor and cassette are not included. OSI 8k BASIC is included in ROM.

The Digital Group Systems 2, 3, and 5. System 2 consists of a Z-80 computer, 16k of RAM, a keyboard, a 9-inch video monitor, and four digital cassette drives. Maxi-BASIC is offered for this system, and it is a particularly powerful version including floating point arithmetic, formatted output, user-defined functions, statement renumbering, and string concatenations. An added bonus is the fact that most source commands (PRINT, FOR, and so on) are stored as single bytes, optimizing the use of memory.

The System 3 is identical to System 2, with the addition of a printer.

SWTPC 6800. The SWTPC 6800 system described in the Tiny BASIC section, when expanded to 8 or preferably 12k of RAM, can support the 8k BASIC described at the beginning of this section.

ASTRAL System I and II

Suite 2
991 Commercial Street
Palo Alto, California 94303

System I is the minimum ASTRAL configuration. It includes ASTRAL BASIC in PROM and 8k of RAM, and it can be upgraded at any time to the other configurations.

System II can be ordered with a plain front panel or full front panel. It includes 32k of RAM and BASIC in PROM. The full front panel—with its switch registers, hexadecimal displays, and clock function—is especially useful in a computer science class, while the expanded memory allows you to run very large programs.

ASTRAL BASIC is standard 8k BASIC with string concatenation and the ability to trace variables and call machine-language subroutines.

HEATHKIT Systems 1, 2, 3 and 4

The Heath Company
Benton Harbor, Michigan 49022

Sold in kit form only, the Heathkit computer systems are based on two processors—the Intel 8080 (used in the H8) and the MOS Technology LSI-11 (used in the H11). The H8 computer includes an 8080 chip, an octal entry keypad on the front panel, a 9-digit octal readout, and the Heath-designed bus. The H11 includes an LSI-11 chip and 4k–32k of RAM; it also includes PDP-11 BASIC and another high-level language, FOCAL, both developed by Digital Equipment Corporation.

System 1 includes the H8, 8k of RAM, a video terminal, and a cassette recorder/player.

System 2, also based on the H8 with 8k of RAM, adds extended BASIC.

System 3 offers the H11 computer with 4k of memory, a video terminal, and a paper tape reader/punch.

System 4, much like System 3, replaces the video terminal with a DECWriter II.

All these systems are available in kit form only.

Tandy TRS-80 (Radio Shack). Level II (8k) BASIC has just been released, and it is a full implementation.

Category Four—Disk BASIC

The next step in sophistication of performance is a faster access to permanently stored data and programs. Many computer systems using an 8K BASIC offer a disk option: Sometimes extended BASIC features are added with this option.

Cromemco System 2D

Cromemco, Inc.
2400 Charleston Road
Mountain View, California 94043

Cromemco System 2D, based on a Z-80 processor, offers a very sophisticated version of BASIC that requires 16k, pre-compiles instructions, has fourteen-digit precision, and offers powerful I/O handling applications. Other software available on the 2D consists of a FORTRAN IV compiler and a Z-80 assembler. Data is stored on 5-inch floppy diskettes, each of which stores 92k of data.

The 2D computer system is available in either kit or assembled and tested form. One disk drive is included, and a second disk drive can be added.

ASTRAL System III. The ASTRAL Dual Floppy Disk System contains 32k of RAM. Each diskette placed in the two disk drives stores about 250,000 characters, and the backsides of some diskettes can be used. Disk BASIC includes all the features of ASTRAL 8k BASIC plus the necessary disk read and write commands. Additional statements allowed are FILES, ASSIGN, CHAIN, COMMON, ADVANCE, and UPDATE. The ASTRAL Monitor and Assembler, included on the Dual Floppy Disk System, makes the ASTRAL System III both an excellent development and instructional system.

The Digital Group Systems 6 and 7. System 6 is similar to System 5, but it offers both disk and tape for mass storage.

System 7 is the same as System 6 but adds a second disk drive.

Special-purpose interfaces are available for such varied uses as ham radio equipment, Votrax voice synthesis, business level BASIC, and word processing equipment.

SOL System 3. The SOL System 3 is a SOL-20 with 48k of memory, a Helios II Model 2 Disk Drive, video monitor, and extended Disk BASIC that adds disk commands to the already powerful 8k BASIC. The SOL System 3, a very powerful computer system, is a good choice in its price range for a full program of educational applications.

Polymorphic System 8813

460 Ward Drive
Santa Barbara, California 93111

The System 8813, based on an 8080 processor and offering a widely varied character set (94 ASCII characters, 32 Greek letters, and special symbols), is another very capable system. The video display offers full-screen cursor control, and a text editor is part of the system software.

Polymorphic's 11k BASIC includes all the scientific functions, multi-line user-defined functions, point-plotting on the video display, formatted output with PRINT USING, a renumber command, and disk read and write commands.

Versatile 2

Computer Data Systems
5460 Fairmont Drive
Wilmington, Delaware 19808

The Versatile 2 is based on a Z-80 CPU, includes a video display with graphics capability, and offers a 12k extended BASIC with disk capability.

COMPAL-80

Computer Power and Light
12321 Ventura Boulevard
Studio City, California 91604

The COMPAL-80, also based on a Z-80 CPU, includes 16k of memory and an extended disk BASIC.

Category Five—Multi-User BASICs

Up in the stratosphere of the microcomputer state-of-the-art are the extremely powerful (but more expensive) multiple disk systems that allow time-sharing. One of these systems is a good choice for a developmental CAI program or for a microcomputer-based administrative software development program. A multi-disk system with at least 32k of memory is roughly comparable to a minicomputer in the late 1960s.

IMSAI VDP-80

IMSAI
14860 Wicks Boulevard
San Leandro, California 94577

The VDP-80 can be used as a remote processor supporting up to six terminals or modems and four tape drives, or it can be used as an intelligent terminal on-line to a larger computer system.

It is based on the Intel 8085 chip, includes 32k of RAM, and supports up to three floppy disk drives that provide up to four megabytes of storage. The standard terminal is a 12-inch CRT, with a programmable font for foreign languages and other special uses. The VDP-80 offers multilingual operation in one of the three languages offered: BASIC, FORTRAN, and DOS. It drives plotters, serial printers, line printers, and practically any special-purpose device.

Cromemco System III. This system, with its Z-80 computer, 32k of RAM, dual disk drives, CRT, and line printer available, provides a similar capability. Memory can be expanded to 512k, and PROM programming is provided on the front panels.

FORTRAN IV (excluding double precision and complex data types) is offered, as is a 16k BASIC (offering extended string handling, PRINT USING, TRACE, integer, single and double precision format, and fourteen-digit precision). The BASIC is *semi-compiled*, which is their term to indicate that each statement is checked for syntax as soon as it is entered, then it is interpreted at run time. A MACRO Assembler and Linking Loader are also parts of the standard software.

Conclusion

Regardless of the equipment you choose—its size, power, or packaging—you are entering a fascinating and rewarding world. Electronic innovations are being welcomed with open arms into many phases of our society. Welcome or not, they are bound to infiltrate the educational world over the next decade. The potential impact in improved student performance and more enthusiastic student participation is astounding.

On the cover of this book, we ask the question, "Will education ever be the same?" We sincerely hope not. Certainly there are many teaching techniques and learning theories from the early days of teaching that should be carefully safeguarded. But it is just as important to merge them with these valuable developments from today's technology in order to attain the greatest gain for the greatest number of students. The merger is a slow and difficult process, but the results are unquestionably worth the effort. We hope you will join us as a participant.

APPENDIX: Comparison of Systems

On the next few pages, the features and prices for the systems described are tabulated for easier comparison. For more detailed product information, write directly to the manufacturer.

	Processor	Memory (Min/Max)	Video Display — Characters/Line	Lines/Page	Character Set	Tiny BASIC (2k-6k)	8k BASIC (8k-12k)	Disk Drive	Time-Sharing	Price
Apple Computer Co. Apple II	6502	4k-48k	40	24	Extensive in 15 colors	In ROM (6k); extended graphics commands	No	No	No	$1,298 (4k) 2,778 (48k)
Radio Shack Tandy TRS-80	Z-80	4k-16k	64	16	Limited	In ROM (4k)	12k BASIC under development	No	No	$ 600 (4k)
The Digital Group System 1	Z-80	10k-32k	Not included			Mini-BASIC on cassette	No	No	No	$1,295 (10k)
System 2	Z-80	18k-32k	Not included			—	Maxi-BASIC with formatted output	No	No	$1,545 (18k)
System 3	Z-80	18k-32k	32	16	Upper and lower case, math, and Greek symbols	—	Renumbering and string concatenation	No	No	$2,545 (18k)
System 5	Z-80	18k-32k	64	16	Upper and lower case, math, and Greek symbols	—	Maxi-BASIC as above	Yes (1 included)	No	$3,995 (18k)
System 6	Z-80	18k-32k	64	16	Upper and lower case, math, and Greek symbols	—	Maxi-BASIC as above	2	No	$4,695
ASTRAL Computer Co. System 1	6800	8k	Not included			—	In PROM and string concatenation	No	No	
System 2	6800	32k	Not included			—	In PROM	No	No	
System 3	6800	32k	Not included			—	On disk	Yes (dual)	No ?	

	Processor	Memory (Min/Max)	Video Display			Tiny BASIC (2k-6k)	8k BASIC (8k-12k)	Disk Drive	Time-Sharing	Price
			Characters/ Line	Lines/ Page	Character Set					
Ohio Scientific Challenger II	6502	16k-192k	32	32	Limited	—	On disk	Single or dual	Up to 4 users (192k)	$1,964 (16k) + disk
Challenger IIP	6502	4k	32 (Monitor not in-cluded)	64	—	—	In ROM	No	No	$ 598
Challenger III	6502A Z-80 6800	32k	(Not included)	64	—	—		Yes		$3,481
Processor Technology SOL System 1	8080	8k	64	16	Upper and lower case	On cassette	No	No	No	$2,095 ($1,600 kit)
SOL System 2	8080	16k	64	16	Upper and lower case		On cassette, very powerful version	No	No	$2,250 ($1,825 kit)
SOL System 3	8080	48k	64	16	Upper and lower case		On cassette, very powerful version	Yes	No	$5,795 (No kit)
Polymorphic Systems System 8813	8080	16k	64	16	Greek and special symbols	—	In ROM, very powerful version	Yes	—	$2,795 (16k & disk)
Cromemco System Z-2	Z-80	None	Not included			—	16k version in PROM	No	No	$ 995 ($ 595 kit)
System Z-2D	Z-80	None	Not included				16k version on disk	Yes	No	$2,095 ($1,495 kit)
System 3	Z-80	32k	80	24			16k version on disk (FORTRAN and Assembler also available)	Yes	Up to 4 users	$5,990 (dual disk drive)

COMPARISON OF SYSTEMS (CONTINUED)

	Processor	Memory (Min/Max)	Video Display			Tiny BASIC (2k-6k)	8k BASIC (8k-12k)	Disk Drive	Time-Sharing	Price
			Characters/Line	Lines/Page	Character Set					
The Heath Co. System 2	8080	8k	80	12	(Monitor not included)		Extended BASIC in ROM	No	No	$1,472 (kit only)
System 3	LSI-11	4k	80	12	(Monitor not included)		BASIC and FOCAL in ROM	No	No	$2,508
Southwest Technical Products SWTPC 6800	6800	4k-32k	32	16	Upper and lower; minimal graphics (Not included)	Available on tape	Available on tape	No	No	$439 (kit only – no monitor or cassette)
Computer Data Systems Versatile 2	Z-80	16k	64	16	Graphics Video display included	—	12k version in ROM	No	No	$2,495
Computer Power and Light COMPAL-80	Z-80	16k	9" monitor included			—	In ROM	No	No	$2,300
IMSAI VDP-80	Intel 8085	32k-192k	80	24	12" CRT included Programmable font (256 special characters)	—	On disk (FORTRAN DOS also available)	Up to 3	Up to 6 users	$5,995 (32k)
Commodore PET	6502	4k-32k	40	25	Upper and lower; 63 graphics characters	—	In ROM; full editing	No	No	$ 595 (4k) $ 795 (8k)

INDEX